Sefer Hayashar

Part I:

From the Creation until Pharaoh's Dreams

Divrei Emes
5776

Yeshiva Beth Moshe Edition

Copyright © 2016 by
by Nachum Y. Kornfeld

All rights reserved. No part of this publication may be reproduced, stored in any retrieval system or transmitted, in any form or by any means, electronic, mechanical, photocopying, recording or otherwise, without permission in writing from the copyright holder.

In many places Sefer Hayashar elucidates and elaborates on the Medrashim brought by Rashi in his commentary on the Torah, in other places it brings from Medrashim which are different than those quoted by Rashi.

Contents

This edition of

Sefer Hayashar

is presented by

Yeshiva Beth Moshe

of Scranton

For over fifty years we have successfully nurtured a generation of dedicated and educated Torah leaders, teachers, and laymen through our high school and Beis Medrash programs.

We are proud of our many alumni who have taken their place serving Hashem for His sake and being *Mekadesh Shem Shomayim.*

May we merit continued success in meeting the challenging educational needs of our times.

Over the years, disseminating valuable, informative and spiritually uplifting Jewish literature has become a tradition at Beth Moshe. It is in this tradition that we proudly present this volume.

Introduction

The discovery of this book was made during the destruction of the holy city of Jerusalem by the wicked Titus. The captains of his armies entered in order to take their spoil of the city. Among them was a general named Sederus. While exploring the city and winding his way through the rubble, he found the remains of what was once a huge mansion. From this building he took everything which he thought to be of value.

As he was about to leave, he noticed what appeared to be something hidden behind a small hole in one of the walls of the mansion. He began to carefully demolish that section of the building when he came upon a huge container full of ancient holy writings. They contained the entire Bible and some historical records of the kings of Israel and of the other nations. He also found manuscripts of the Mishnah, and many other holy scrolls. As he proceeded further into this secret bunker, he found a well-stocked pantry containing food and wine.

Sederus then noticed an old man, alone in a secluded chamber, who was studying other ancient books. The general was taken aback by this amazing sight. He spoke softly to the old scholar. “Why do you sit alone among these ruins without anyone to keep you company?”

“I have known for many years,” the man replied, “that the Holy City would be destroyed. I built this house with an underground passage leading to this chamber through which I brought all these books. I thought that I would thus preserve my own life.”

God caused the general to take pity on the old man and Sederus took the scholar along on his journeys until they reached the city of Seville in Spain. The general was so impressed with the man’s knowledge of so many subjects that he made him stay with him and became his student. He built a large house outside Seville and there they wrote down all the events which would happen until the coming of Mashiach.

So it was that when God violently drove us into exile by the hand of the king of Edom, and expelled us from city to city and from country to country in our sad condition, there came into our possession a book known as Toldos Adam (the Generations of Adam [or Man]) together with many other works. These came to us at the city called Napoli (Naples), then ruled by the king of Spain. When we saw that these volumes were full of wisdom, we decided to print them for publication as we did with all books of which we approve. This, however, was the most important of them all. There are twelve editions of this work and not one varied in any way from the other in spelling or context.

We realized that there was great spiritual value in these books so we set about the task of having them printed. The original title of the book is *Sefer Hayashar.* It was given this title since its contents are arranged in a strictly chronological order. No earlier event is made to follow a later one, and no later one to precede the earlier. This justifies the title which means "The Correct or *Right* Book." It used to be called the *Book of the Generations of Adam,* but the correct title is, as we have said, *Sefer Hayashar.* This is also the title which the Greek Jews give it, *Libros de los Falabros* (in Ladino, spoken by the Jews of Salonika).

In the Book of Chashmoneans we are told that King Ptolemy of Egypt ordered his servants to collect the legal writings of all peoples. His purpose was to establish a perfect order of justice for all. They collected a total of nine hundred and sixty-five tomes, but he wished to make the number one thousand. Thereupon certain evil sinners of the People of Israel said, "Oh king, why all this toil? Send to Jerusalem and order the Jews to bring you their Torah written by the word of God through the prophets. In this way, you will learn great wisdom." He took their advice, but the Jews were reluctant to comply. Instead they sent the king the *Sefer Hayashar.* King Ptolemy was pleased with it. He then abandoned the study of all the other books and blessed the person who advised him to obtain this volume.

In time, these evil sinners discovered that the real Torah was never sent to the king. They informed the king, who became very angry, and he sent word to Jerusalem once more to obtain a copy of the Torah itself. This time he took precautions and sent for seventy elders whom he received and placed in seventy separate rooms. Each one was ordered to render his independent translation of the Torah (into Greek). The Divine spirit came upon them and they all rendered the version in exactly the same manner without the slightest variation. Ptolemy was very happy and showed great appreciation to the scholars who translated the Torah.

When Ptolemy died, the Jews used ingenuity to rescue this version, but they did leave the *Sefer Hayashar* with his son. This served to show each successive ruler that God had chosen Israel and that there is none beside God. The book is still in Egypt and copies reached all the countries of the exile, and as was stated above, it found its way to the city Napoli, ruled by the King of Spain.

You will, therefore, dear reader, find here some accounts concerning the kings of Edom and Crete and even Africa. This is not the principal purpose of the work, but it is important to make known to all, the difference between the wars of Israel and those of the heathens. The victories of Israel are not those of chance, but of miracle. These events alone teach us to place our trust in Him.

Therefore, you will see that the purposes of this book are numerous. They all lead us to the idea of faith in God and of clinging to Him and His ways. The first purpose is the knowledge we gain of the facts of Creation and the first twenty generations of man. The second is the additional material surrounding the birth of our father, Avraham, and his clinging to God and of his conflict with King Nimrod. It includes the story of the Age of Dispersion (Tower of Bavel) and how the people were scattered to the ends of the earth. It tells of the building of the cities and states. The third purpose is that we learn about the attachment of our forefathers to God. The fourth is the story of the wicked cities, Sodom and Amora, and their destruction. This will teach us to keep far from sin. The fifth reason is that we have recorded here the devotion of Yitzchak and Yaakov to God and the prayer of our mother, Sarah, and the binding of Yitzchak. This teaches us to incline our hearts to His service.

Next, the story of events describing the wars of the Sons of Yaakov with Shechem and the other cities should arouse in us the virtue of trust. In seventh place, the telling of the full story of Yoseif in Egypt and Potifar and his wife and the king of Egypt moves us to fear God. In eighth place, we are informed of the deeds of Moshe in Ethiopia and in Midian. This alone will show us how God works with the righteous. In ninth place, we are given many details of the slavery of Israel in Egypt — how this began and how they were subjected to all manner of bondage. One should read this section on the evenings of Pesach, especially after the Seder. This, in fact, is the practice in Spain. After we end the Seder, we read all the events from the descent into Egypt up to the deliverance.

In tenth place, some of the comments of our sages, of blessed memory, will be found in this book, such as the story of the angels who met Yaakov when he returned from Mesopotamia. The eleventh reason is that we are told about the story of the angel, Gavriel, who taught Yoseif seventy languages and the explanation of the verse "Who slew Midian in the field of Moav" (Bereishis 36:35). The twelfth reason is that any person who is called upon to preach in public may use this material which is not found elsewhere.

There is a thirteenth and final thought. There are traveling merchants and wayfarers who may find here a condensed form of Torah study and thus benefit spiritually. It gives a pleasure to the mind and the thoughts since it contains countless stories, as we have said, which are not told elsewhere.

All the above reasons being considered, it was thought commendable to print and publish this book. It will receive recognition throughout the communities of Israel. This will induce us to ponder on the wonders of God and His mercies and those which he performed for our fathers; that He chose us out of all the peoples. So that by this study, we will learn to fear God. We put our trust in God on Whom we lean and we ask Him to help us in the fulfillment of this task, which is the work of heaven. We pray to Him to grant us success and to guide us in the right path, to deliver us from mistakes and absolve us from hidden errors. This is how King David prayed in Tehillim "Who can understand errors, so clear us from hidden things" (*Tehillim*). May God show us the good way and lead us in the path of success for the sake of His mercies and kindnesses and may He grant the requests of our hearts for good, Amen, and may it be His will . . .

Bereishis

The Creation of Man

This is the book of generations of *Adam* whom God created pon the earth on the day that God made earth and heaven. God said, "Let us make man in Our image and in Our likeness." Then God formed the man from the ground. God blew into him the breath of life and man became a living soul with the power of speech.

God said, "It is not good for a man to be alone so I shall make for him a compatible helper." God then caused Adam to fall into a deep sleep. As Adam slept, God removed one of his ribs and, having built flesh around it to form Chava, brought her to man. Adam awoke and found the woman standing before him. He thought, "This is bone of my bones. She will be called woman (*ishah*) since she was taken from man (*ish*)." He named her Chava as she was the mother of all living humans.

God blessed them and called them *Adam* on the day when man was created. God said, "Be fruitful and multiply and fill the earth." He took Adam and his wife and placed them in *Gan Eiden* (the Garden of Eden) to till it and to watch over it. He commanded them, "You may eat of all the trees of the Garden, but from the Tree of Knowledge of Good and Evil you may not eat, since on the day you eat of it you will surely die." Then, having blessed them, He ascended.

Adam and his wife lived in that Garden as God had commanded. But God had created the serpent on earth. Now this serpent came to tempt them to transgress the command which they had received. With great cunning the serpent beguiled the woman to eat of the fruit of the Tree of Knowledge. She listened to it and took some of the fruit of that tree and gave of it to her husband too. By transgressing that commandment, they aroused God's anger and He cursed them and banished them from the Garden. They would now work, with anguish, the ground from which they were taken. They left the Garden and dwelt east of Eiden.

KAYIN AND HEVEL

Adam lived with his wife and she gave birth to two sons and three daughters. The elder son was named Kayin which implies acquiring a son (with God's help). The younger one was called Hevel which means "nothing," as if to say we came with nothing and we shall leave this earth with nothing.

The lads grew and their father gave them both possession of a piece of land. Kayin tilled the soil and Hevel became a shepherd. After a time they both brought an offering to God. Kayin brought some of the fruit of the earth and Hevel brought the firstborn of his sheep, selected from the best he had. So God was attentive to Hevel and to his gift and a fire came down from heaven and consumed the offering. But God paid no regard to the gift of Kayin, as he had given only the worst of his fruit. Kayin became jealous of his brother and began to seek a means of destroying him.

One day both brothers came to do their work as usual. Kayin plowed and Hevel tended his sheep. It happened that some sheep passed by the field where Kayin was plowing. Kayin became infuriated and turned to Hevel and said in an angry voice, "Why have you brought your sheep to graze on my land?" Hevel replied, "In that case, why do you eat the meat of my lambs and use their fleece for the wool of your clothing? Remove your woolen clothes and pay for all the meat you have eaten! If you do this, I shall leave your land, never to come back." Kayin, burning with hatred, said, "If I were to kill you now who would seek revenge from me?" Hevel calmly replied, "The God who created us to live on this earth will avenge my blood. God is Judge and He will render to man evil for evil and He will do to the wicked according to his evil ways. Should you slay me, be assured that God will know your hiding place and He will judge you for the evil which you plan."

When Kayin heard these words he flew into a rage, and, flushed with anger, raised the plowing iron and killed his brother. Hevel's blood streamed in torrents before the sheep, soaking the ground. Kayin, at the sight of his fallen brother, regretted his evil deed, and wept bitterly. With a heavy heart he dug a hole in the ground, and hid the body by covering it with earth.

But God knew what had happened and he called to Kayin, "Where is your brother Hevel?" Kayin answered, "I do not know, am I my brother's keeper?" God continued, "What have you done? The sound of your brother's voice cries to Me from the earth. You have killed your brother and you even believed that I would not see your act. You killed him because he spoke truthfully to you. Now you will be cursed from the very ground which opened itself to take your brother's blood and into which you buried him. When you till that earth, it will not continue to yield its full strength for you. There will grow thorns and thistles and you will be a wanderer and a fugitive in the world."

Kayin left God's presence and wandered about the earth east of Eiden with his belongings. He had a son whom he called Chanoch which contains the meaning of "ease," since God began to give him ease and tranquility. At this time Kayin began to build a city which he named after his son Chanoch. It was also at this time that God gave Kayin some repose so that he was not made to wander about so much. To Chanoch was born Irad and to Irad was born Mechuyo'el and to Mechuyo'el was born Mesusho'el and Mesusho'el had a son called Lemech.

The Ten Generations

It happened in the one hundred and thirtieth year of the life of Adam that he resumed living with his wife and she bore him a son in his likeness and form. She called him Sheis meaning that God had replaced the lost brother Hevel who had been killed by Kayin. When Sheis was one hundred and five years old he had a son whom he named Enosh. This name implies that a time had come when men began to multiply, to bring pain to their own souls and to bring God's anger on them by rebelling against Him. Men began to worship other gods and to forget about God who had created them. They formed images of iron and wood and worshiped them. So in the time of Enosh, men forsook God.

God's anger was kindled against them because of their abominations. He brought a flood from the waters of the River Gichon which destroyed a third of the earth. The seed which they sowed grew into thorns and briers. The earth had already been cursed since Adam's sin and now it became worse in its deterioration.

Enosh was ninety when his son Keinan was born. When Keinan was forty, he was already so wise that he had mastered many subjects and he ruled over the spirits and the demons. Keinan indeed knew that God was about to destroy mankind because of their sinful lives. There would be a destructive flood in due time. Keinan wrote these things on tablets of stone and placed them in his treasury. Keinan ruled over the entire earth and restored many people to the right path of life.

When Keinan was seventy he had three sons and two daughters. The oldest son was named Mehalalel, the second Einan, and the third Mered. Their sisters were Adah and Tzillah. Lemech, the son of Mesusha'el arranged for marriages of his children into the family of Keinan whose two daughters became Lemech's wives. Lemech had a son by Adah whom he called Yaval and another son whom he named Yuval. The other wife, Tzillah, Adah's sister, was barren. It was the practice in those days to trespass the command, "be fruitful and multiply." Some men gave their wives a potion which rendered them unable to bear children. This was done in order to preserve their beauty. Tzillah was one of these. Those who bore children were treated by their husbands with some contempt, whereas the ones rendered barren were favorites. Yet, it transpired that towards old age Tzillah, too, conceived. She called her son Tuval Kayin. This was a play on words meaning, "now that I am old and worn out I gained him from God." She then gave birth to a daughter whom she called Na'amoh. This word means "pleasure." She referred to the fact that at that age she was granted this pleasure.

The Accident

At this time Lemech was very old and his sight began to fail. He was attended by his son Tuval Kayin. One day, father and son went hunting in the field. Kayin, Adam's son, happened to be in the vicinity, but Lemech could not see him. Tuval Kayin asked his father, Lemech, to draw the bow since he saw Kayin at a distance and thought that the latter was a wild animal. The arrow pierced Kayin and killed him. The curse for Kayin's murder of Hevel, his brother, was thus fulfilled.

Then Lemech and his little son went to examine the body of the fallen prey. As they approached, they discovered that it was their own ancestor Kayin. Lemech was so shocked and horrified at this accident that, in despair, he clapped his hands. Tuval Kayin was caught between his father's hands and was killed instantly by the blow.

Lemech's wives heard about this tragic event and, overcome with grief, planned to kill him. They hated him for the rest of his days. Repelled by the old man's presence, they deserted him until he prevailed upon them to listen to him.

Trembling with emotion Lemech said, "Adah and Tzillah, wives of Lemech, give ear to my statement. You believe that I killed a man by wounding him and a child by smiting for no reason at all! Don't you know that I am very old and I acted without foreknowledge?" His wives were moved by his words and returned to him. But they did not bear him any more children, for they realized that the anger of God was growing against mankind. All men were to be destroyed by a disastrous flood in retribution for their evil and corrupt ways.

CHANOCH

Now Mehalalel, the son of Keinan, was sixty-five years old when he had a son, Yered. Yered was one hundred and sixty-two years old when he had a son named Chanoch. Chanoch was sixty-five years old when he had a son, Mesushelach. Chanoch walked in God's path after his son was born. He served Him and rejected the evil ways of his contemporaries. His soul clung to God's teachings with knowledge and insight so that he knew all the ways of God. He left the company of men because of his wisdom, and he went into seclusion for a long time. After many years of living in this fashion and praying to God in isolation, an angel of God called to him, saying, "Chanoch, Chanoch," and the latter replied, "I am here."

The angel said to Chanoch, "Get up and leave your seclusion and return to society to rule over them. You will teach them the right ways and the proper deeds which they should perform."

Chanoch, greatly agitated by the angel's call, stirred into action. He gathered people around him and taught them about God. Word was sent around everywhere announcing that whoever wanted to know the ways of God and the good life should come to Chanoch for instruction. Hungry for the truth, people eagerly gathered around him and he taught them the wisdom of God. Thus the people served God all the lifetime of Chanoch. Rulers, princes, and judges, all came to hear him. He was loved and respected so much that three hundred rulers proclaimed him king over them. With gentle persuasion he was able to establish peaceful relations between all these rulers. He reigned for two hundred and forty-three years, guiding all people in the ways of God.

These were the sons of Chanoch. Mesushelach, Elishua, Elimelech — three sons, and two daughters — Malkoh and Na'amoh. When Mesushelach was one hundred and eighty-seven years old he had a son, Lemech. It was in the fifty-sixth year of Lemech's life that Adam died at the age of nine hundred and thirty. At the behest of God, Adam's son, Sheis, and his sons, and Chanoch and Mesushelach buried Adam with great honor in the Cave of the Kings. Everyone mourned him with tears and much sorrow, a practice which has been preserved for all men to this day. Adam died because he had transgressed the command of God in eating from the Tree of Knowledge.

It was in the two hundred and fifty-third year of Chanoch's reign that Adam died. Chanoch decided to go into seclusion again and to live in solitude as he had done previously. He actually carried out his plan, except that he did not absent himself all the time. He would isolate himself for three days at a time, then present himself for one day. During the three days he devoted himself to his own spiritual exercises and on the fourth he taught as before. This became his continual practice. After a time, he would disappear for six days at a time and appear for only one day (on the seventh). Then it changed to an appearance of one day each month and finally, only one day each year. Everyone implored him to return to them, but they could not move him. They revered him greatly and were afraid to approach him on account of the Divine Presence which was on his countenance. They feared that they might perish because of his radiant appearance.

Kings from far and wide met and took counsel and presented themselves before Chanoch. When he consented to resume his daily instruction the kings joyfully shouted in unison: "Long live the king!" It happened that during one of the sessions an angel appeared to him, saying, "It is my wish to take you to Heaven where you shall reign over the angels just as you have done among men." Upon hearing this awesome message, Chanoch summoned all the inhabitants of the earth and taught them the wisdom of God. He said, "I have been commanded to ascend to Heaven but I do not know the day of my departure so let me teach you while I may, before I depart for all time."

He lived among them for some days and taught them. Then, one day while he was teaching, they saw the form of a huge horse descending from heaven, running as swiftly as the wind. Chanoch told them, "This horse has come for me. The time has come for me to leave you." A proclamation was issued. "Whoever wishes to study with Chanoch must come to him at once." Then he instructed them for the last time and also made peace between them.

Now he arose and mounted his horse. He was followed by eight hundred thousand men for a distance of one day's journey. On the second day he said, "You must return to your homes lest you perish." Nevertheless, some insisted on remaining, but he continued to warn them each day to leave him. On the sixth day he spoke to them again warning them to leave. Many left but some remained and tearfully said, "Where you go, we shall go, and only death shall separate us." Chanoch now desisted from his warnings and the kings took a count to see how many had remained of them.

On the seventh day, before an awe-stricken crowd of admirers, Chanoch ascended to Heaven in a whirlwind with fiery horses and fiery chariots. The kings rushed to that very spot and found it covered with snow. On the snow they found a mass of huge boulders of ice. They attempted to break through the iceblocks to see if anyone was buried beneath. Their efforts were fruitless and they sadly concluded that all those who had remained with Chanoch had perished. They searched for Chanoch but he was never found, for he had ascended to Heaven. He had lived for three hundred and sixty-five years.

It was in the hundred and thirteenth year of the life of Lemech's son Mesushelach, that Chanoch ascended to Heaven. At this time, all the kings of the earth came to Mesushelach, asking him to reign over them, and thus he was crowned as their king. Mesushelach did all that was upright, as his father, Chanoch, had done before him. At the end of his life, however, men began to rebel against God. In retaliation, God destroyed the seed of the earth and there was no harvest. The ground grew thistles. Yet the people did not repent of their evil ways and were bent on wrongdoing. God was angry. He regretted that He had created man and now planned to obliterate them.

THE BIRTH OF NOACH

When Lemech was one hundred and sixty years old, Sheis, Adam's son died. He had lived for nine hundred and twelve years. When Lemech was eighty-one years old he took for a wife Eshmoa, daughter of Elishua, son of Chanoch, his uncle. In those days men sowed the earth but found little food. Even so, they did not turn from their evil ways and they rebelled against their Creator. Lemech's wife conceived and bore him a son. His grandfather, Mesushelach, called him Noach implying that the land had begun to rest and was not being spoiled as before. Lemech, his father, called him Menachem stating, as the Torah says, "This one will comfort us from our work and from the toil of our hands from the earth which God cursed."

The boy grew up and walked in the ways of his grandfather, Mesushelach. He was perfect in his observance of the ways of God. But mankind had turned away from those ways. As they multiplied with sons and daughters, each man taught his children evil ways. Each man fashioned his own god, and they robbed and were violent. The whole earth was full of violence. Their judges and police officers abducted young girls and forcibly robbed men of their wives, whenever they chose to. Even the beasts of the field, the wild animals, and birds were taught to behave unnaturally. All this was done to provoke God.

God saw that the earth was corrupt. Every form of life had perverted its way on earth — man and beast. God said, "I will blot out mankind which I have created from the face of the earth — man, bird and beast — for I regret that I created them." Every man who did walk in God's ways died in those days before God brought the evil which He had promised to bring. This was done by God so that they would not have to witness the destruction which He had decided to bring upon the earth.

Only Noach found favor in God's eyes. God chose him and his sons in order to preserve life on the face of the earth.

Noach

It was in the eighty-fourth year of the life of Noach that Enosh, the son of Sheis, died at the age of nine hundred and five. Keinan, the son of Enosh, died in the one hundred and seventy-ninth year of Noach's life. Keinan lived for nine hundred and ten years. In the two hundred and thirty-fourth year of the life of Noach, Mehalalel, the son of Keinan, died. Mehalalel lived for eight hundred and ninety-five years. At that time, Yered, the son of Mehalalel died. This was in the three hundred and sixty-sixth year of the life of Noach. Yered lived for nine hundred and two years. It so happened that those men who had followed God wholeheartedly died during this period. This was so that they should not see the evil which God had threatened to bring on the earth.

Announcing the Great Flood

By the four hundred and eightieth year of Noach's life, all those good people had died. Only Mesushelach was left of the old generation. It was then that God told Mesushelach and Noach to proclaim to all the world as follows: "Thus says God. Repent of your evil ways and He will change the decree He has made against you." Obediently, both these men proclaimed this warning to all. This they did day after day, but people refused to take heed. Now God set a deadline of one hundred and twenty years. This gave them further opportunity to repent, and God then would likewise withdraw His plan of destruction.

Owing to this impending doom, Noach, refrained from marrying and having children. He thought that if God were to destroy the earth, he would not like to bring children into such a fate. But he was a righteous man and God wished to preserve him and mankind through the children he might have. It was planned that Noach and his children would survive. So in obedience to God's purpose, he chose a wife. She was Na'amah, the daughter of

Chanoch, and she was five hundred and eighty years old. Their first son was named Yefes which implies enlargement, as if to say, "God has enlarged us and wishes to make a room for mankind through us." The second son was named Shem which is taken from the word *sam,* to place or to make ready. This implied that preparation was being made for the future of mankind. Noach was now five hundred and two years old.

These lads grew up and walked in God's path. They had been well trained by Mesushelach and by Noach. Lemech, Noach's father, died at the age of seven hundred and seventy-seven but he had not walked in God's ways completely. This happened in the five hundred and ninety-fifth year of Noach's life.

The Great Flood

After repeated warnings to men, God said, "The end of all living things has come before Me on account of their evil deeds and I plan to destroy them from the face of the earth. So get cypress wood and build a huge ark and let it stand there." This ark was to be three hundred cubits in length; fifty in width and thirty in height. "Make a door at the side and make the top of the ark slanted by sloping it to a width of one cubit at the top. Cover it inside and outside with pitch. Then I will bring a flood on the earth to destroy all life. Everything on the earth will perish. You must gather all the animals, male and female, so as to preserve life on the earth. All type of food suitable for each species must be stored in it. Choose three women for your sons so that they marry."

In the five hundred and ninety-fifth year of his life, Noach began to build the ark, and took the three daughters of Eliakim, the son of Mesushelach, as wives for his three sons. It was at this point that Mesushelach, the son of Chanoch, died at the age of nine hundred and sixty-nine.

God now told Noach, "Enter the ark with your family. All the animals will be brought to you and will surround the ark." Noach was to go and place himself at the entrance and all these animals would present themselves to him. All those who would kneel before him were to be admitted, but those who remained in standing posture would be left outside. Noach acted accordingly, admitting only those which knelt.

Just then, a she lion presented herself with her two whelps, male and female. The three of them kneeled before Noach. Suddenly, the two young lions attacked their mother sinking their sharp claws and fangs into her flesh. The mother fled and sought refuge among other lions nearby. Noach was very puzzled by this scene, but he took the two young ones into the ark. Of the clean animals, he took seven pairs, male and female.

For the next seven days no rain appeared. Then threatening black clouds appeared with thunderbolts and flashes of lightning accompanied by such a terrifying noise as had never been heard before. This was really the final warning to make men repent, yet they remained stubborn.

After these seven days, in the six hundredth year of the life of Noach, the flood began with all its fierceness. The fountains of the Great Depth were opened as well as the flood gates of heaven, and the downpour continued for forty days. God had sealed Noach safely in the ark. When it became obvious that the rain was abnormally heavy, men began to cry out to Noach to let them enter. A crowd of 700,000 people had now gathered around the ark. Noach admonished them, "Did you not rebel against God and did I not warn you. You even denied His existence. I cautioned you for the past one hundred and twenty years and now you suddenly change your mind because your life is in danger!"

They begged for another chance to repent but they had been given so many warnings that it was now too late. They then attempted to break down the ark's door, but the animals which remained outside attacked them — some were killed while others managed to escape from these beasts. Eventually all living things died — beasts, birds and even creeping things. The occupants of the ark were tossed about violently until Noach prayed to God. Then a wind came and the waters began to subside. The well-springs of the deep and the floodgates of heaven were now closed. The waters receded and the ark finally rested on ground.

Then Noach prayed, "Oh God of the whole universe, take me out of this enclosure. I am weary of my groaning." Then God revealed to him that only after a full year would he be allowed to leave.

The year passed and the earth was indeed dry. Noach removed the cover of the ark on the seventh day of the second month. He left the ark only when he was commanded by God to do so. When they finally left, each being went its own way. Noach and his family stayed in the land which he was told to inherit. He served God all his life as before. God blessed them saying, "Be fruitful and multiply and fill the whole earth."

NIMROD

The third son of Noach was named Cham who had a son named Kush. Kush married and had a son whom he called Nimrod. The very name suggested rebellion (*marad*). Nimrod's father had given to him the skin-coats which God had made for Adam and Chavah when they were expelled from the Garden of Eiden. When Adam died these garments were passed on to Chanoch, the son of Yered, and then to his son, Mesushelach. Then Noach took them and brought them to the ark where they were kept until they left that enclosure. Cham stole these garments and hid them from his father and brothers. Later he gave them to his son, Kush, who hid them until his son, Nimrod, was born.

Nimrod was twenty years old when he first donned this coat. When wearing it, he sensed a surge of strength and energy. He became a mighty hunter and killed animals which he offered to God as a sacrifice. He even fought wars on his brothers' behalf and subdued all of his enemies. It became a proverb in those days that when anyone trained soldiers he would say to them, "Be as Nimrod who is a mighty hunter in the land."

When Nimrod was forty years old a war broke out between his brothers and the sons of Yefes. Nimrod gathered the sons of Kush and the sons of Cham and came to the aid of his brothers. Together, these warriors subdued their mighty enemies. The enemies' sons were taken as hostages and used as slaves.

Nimrod, being victorious, was now made king, and he made Terach, the son of Nachor, his chief captain. Then he took counsel with his officers about building a city as the royal capital. In their search for a suitable site they came across a plain where they built a magnificent metropolis, which they named Shin'ar. Nimrod ruled all mankind with an iron fist, so that his fame spread throughout the world.

All people heard about his greatness and they brought him gifts and paid homage to him. Many people now settled in the region of Shin'ar.

At this time the earth's peoples spoke the same language with uniform words. They did not walk in the ways of God but were as wicked as the men in the time of the flood. Nimrod also taught men his own evil ways and made gods of wood and stone. His son, Mardan, was even worse than his father, as it says, "From the wicked there proceeds wickedness" (Shmuel 24:13).

Avram's Birth

Terach was the son of Nachor and was captain of Nimrod's armies. He married Amasla, the daughter of Karnavo. Amasla gave birth to a son when Terach was seventy years old. This son was named Avram. The king had promoted Terach at that time and the name Avram indicated his high position (*ram*). When this child was born, Nimrod's entire court assembled to celebrate the event at the house of Terach. That night, as they left the banquet, they noticed a peculiar scene in the skies. A great star had risen in the east which seemed to swallow four other stars from the four points of the compass. The wise men said, "This is an evil omen for Nimrod. It points to the future of the child, Avram. He will be a very mighty ruler and through his descendants he will conquer the world."

The ministers and wise men were very worried and began to discuss the matter among themselves. They reasoned, "If we conceal this information from Nimrod, and he discovers the truth of the scene, he will accuse us of hiding it from him and he will kill us."

They decided to tell Nimrod how they had been banqueting with Terach and upon departing had seen a wondrous heavenly scene. The chief magician added, "This celestial event portends great danger for you, great king, and for many mighty rulers." They continued, "This new-born child, Avram, is a threat to us all. We advise you to arrest the child for the safety of all and to remove this menace from our midst." Nimrod summoned Terach and offered him a huge sum of money in order to let him have the child. His plan was, of course, to kill Avram.

Terach, standing before Nimrod resolutely said, "Your Majesty, permit me to relate to you an incident that occurred only last night. Ayon, the son of Marad, came to me and asked me to sell him the fine stallion which you had given me as a gift. He offered me much gold for it but I said I would ask the king about this first." Nimrod, taken aback, replied, "Are you so foolish as to think of parting with such a gift? To barter a proud horse, the like of which is not to be found in the whole land?"

Terach, looking the king straight in the eye, said, "You, oh king, have asked me to do the same thing by asking me to trade my own son for money. What use have I for gold if my son is taken from me? I will have no one to inherit me and the gold will revert to the king."

But Nimrod would not be put off by such logic and angrily insisted. Terach thought of a plan. He asked, "Give me three days to think the matter over." Nimrod, knowing very well that he could have Avram brought to him by force, granted Terach's wish. After three days, Nimrod sent word to Terach and again offered him the sum he had promised for his son. "If you refuse," the message read, "you and your entire household will be destroyed."

Terach now put his plan into action. He took one of his servant's children, which had been born at that very time. (This child was indeed the son of Terach by a maidservant and was born on the same day as Avram.) Terach gave Nimrod this child and received the reward. The matter was forgotten after Nimrod had the child killed. Avram was taken by his parents and hidden in a remote cave, with a nurse to care for him. Avram grew and God was with him. He remained in that cave for ten years.

At this time Haran, son of Terach and brother of Avram, married. His wife gave birth to a son whom he named Lot. Haran was thirty-nine years old when this son was born. Then Haran had another child, a daughter called Milkah and then a daughter called Sarai. When Haran was forty-two years old, Avram was ten years old. When Avram left the cave, he journeyed to Noach and his son, Shem, and lived in their home and studied the ways of God. No one knew of Avram's existence and Avram lived with Noach and Shem for a long time.

Avram now acknowledged the true God and had been with his teachers for thirty-nine years. Indeed, already at the age of three, Avram had followed God's ways. He did so until the end of his life.

All men again rebelled against God. They made their own gods of wood and stone. Terach and his household likewise practiced idolatry. He had twelve such idols, one for each month of the year. Only Noach and his household remained faithful to God.

Avram Finds God

Avram had learned much wisdom and refused to accept the folly of worshiping man-made gods. He originally discovered God in the following manner. One day he looked at the sun and realized that this huge body gave light to the world and he thought, "This radiant sun warms and sustains the world — it must be God. I will worship it and pray to it. But in the evening the sun set and Avram said, "No, the sun cannot be the true God." Then he watched the appearance of the moon and stars at night and he said, "These must be the Gods who created man and his world. I will bow down to them." But they all disappeared when the hour of sunnnrise arrived. He concluded, "None of these can possibly be the Creator. They are merely servants of the Almighty God." So Avram, when returning to the house of Noach, remained a faithful worshiper of God. The world, however, was still evil and Nimrod reigned securely.

THE TOWER OF BAVEL

As has already been mentioned, the whole of mankind spoke one language with uniform words. All the princes and Mitzraim, Kush and Canaan took counsel together and said, "Let us build a city and a tower in its midst as a fortress reaching to the sky. We shall become very famous and no enemy will be able to hurt us. We shall never be scattered all over the earth." Nimrod took this advice and gathered together 600,000 men and sought out a wide territory on which to build this city. After searching for two years they found a suitable valley to the east of Shinar. Then they constructed furnaces in which to cast bricks. Their plan was an evil one because their purpose was to make war against God, climbing to the heavens to do battle.

Now there were differences of opinion as to how to attain victory. One group said, "Let us ascend and fight." Another said, "Let us place our own gods in heaven" and the third said, "We shall use weapons to shoot at God Himself." It took a year to get the bricks and mortar to the top, where the builders were waiting to receive the materials. There was constant ascending and descending. If a brick fell and was lost, everyone wept, but if a human life was lost, nobody cared. The arrows which they began to shoot upwards returned to them dripping with blood. They believed that they were really killing celestial beings.

Years passed and God said to seventy angels, “Let us descend and confuse their speech so that no one will understand the meaning of his co-worker.” Instantly, they forgot their common language and they failed to understand one another. If one man said to the other, “Give me a stone,” the other gave him mortar. When he received mortar instead of a brick, he threw it back, killing the person who had handed it to him. A great number of laborers met their death in this manner.

The result was mass confusion and the project came to an abrupt end. God took vengeance on the three groups. Those who said, “Let us ascend and fight,” became apes and elephants. The group who said, “Let us place our own gods in heaven” were killed by one another’s hand. And those who said, “We shall make war with God” were scattered over the face of the earth. The remainder fled and were likewise dispersed over the whole world. The work of building ceased. The name of the place was now Bavel since God had confused their language.

As to the tower itself, a third of its height was swallowed into the earth, a third was burned and the other third is there to this day. Part of it is also suspended in mid air and casts its shadow over a distance of three days travel. Peleg, son of Ever, died at this time in the forty-eighth year of Avram’s life. Peleg lived two hundred and thirty-nine years (Peleg implies division).

Now that men were scattered over the face of the entire earth, they built cities wherever they settled and gave these cities names. Many of these cities were named after themselves or after their sons.

Nimrod, son of Kush, while still in the land of Shinar, had built cities. One was Bavel, one Erech, one Akkad and a fourth called Kalneh. Here his ambitions came to an end and many rebelled against him. Nimrod remained in Bavel where he established a kingdom. He was now renamed Amrafel. This word implies a meaning of fallen. He did not repent of his idolatrous practices and his son remained as wicked as ever, even worse than his father. This son was Mardan.

At this time a war was fought between the families of Cham's children. Kedorlaomer, King of Elam, left the descendants of Cham. He had conquered the whole domain of Cham and he then went to the five cities on the plain and subdued them. They paid tribute to him for twelve years. At that time Nachor, the son of Serug died. This was in the forty-ninth year of the life of Avram. Nachor had lived for one hundred and forty-eight years. In the fiftieth year of his life, Avram left the house of Noach and returned to his father, Terach. Terach was still the chief captain of Nimrod's army.

Avram Destroys the Idols

Avram came to Terach's house and saw twelve idols, each placed in its own temple. Avram became very angry and he said to himself, "With God's help, I will demolish these idols before three days will have passed." Seething with fury, he rushed to his father who was seated in the outer courtyard with his servants. Avram, fuming with indignation, burst out, "Tell me, father, where is the God Who created Heaven and Earth, and Who made you and me?" Terach, with a puzzled look in his eyes replied, "They are right here," and he led him into the chambers where the idols were kept. There were twelve large ones and countless minor ones. Filled with loathing and disgust, Avram stared at the collection of idols — big and small — as Terach reverently said, "These gods created me and you and all that is in the world." Terach then bowed down to these images.

Then Avram went to his mother and asked her, "Please prepare a succulent goat as a sacrifice to my father's gods." She prepared a delectable dish which Avram put before one of the idols. He left the food there, but, of course, it was not eaten or touched. Avram scoffed at this and he remarked, "Perhaps they did not like the food, or it was not sufficient, and because of this they rejected the offering." So he asked for better dishes. The idols did not like these any better.

That night the spirit of God embraced Avram and he called out, "Woe is me, for my father and this entire evil generation which turns towards this folly. They worship idols who cannot hear or see." Entered these chambers he took an ax, and, swinging left and right, blow after lightning blow, he obliterated the idols and left them in shambles. He left the largest one untouched and placed the ax in its hand. When his father heard the noise of the destruction, he entered and found Avram leaving.

Terach entered the chamber of the idols, and seeing the shattered idols, he rushed to Avram. Fuming with rage he exploded: "Avram, what have you done to my idols?" Avram calmly answered, "On the contrary; I placed an offering before them. All the idols hungrily reached for the food, so the big one took an ax and cut them down. You see, he is still holding the ax in his hand." Terach, pounding his fist on the table shouted, "You are lying. This cannot be true. Idols have no such power to smash things." Then Avram said, "How can you be so senseless as to worship a god who cannot even save himself? How will he help you or answer your prayer? You have forgotten the God who created heaven and earth and who created you. You bring great wrong upon your soul and you have forgotten how the earth was punished for such crimes. Dear father, turn away from your sinful acts, for they will lead you and your family to ruin." Then Avram completed the work. He took the ax and broke the huge idol which was left.

Avram Confronts Nimrod

Terach rushed to the royal palace and told Nimrod, "I must reveal to you, Your Majesty, that fifty years ago a son was born to me. Now this son has destroyed all my idols." Nimrod sent three officers to bring Avram to him. Nimrod was holding court and

Terach was present. When he was questioned, Avram told the same story to the king, about the quarrel among the idols. The king ridiculed the description given by Avram.

Avram boldly confronted Nimrod, "How can you place your trust in a god who cannot even save himself?" Raising his voice, his eyes flashing, he continued, "Why do you mislead everyone, you perverse and foolish leader. Instead of showing the true way to your servants, you fill the earth with sin. Such acts brought destruction to the earth and you will bring evil on yourselves and the world. Remove this evil practice from yourselves at once. Serve God in Whose hand is your life and you will prosper. If not, you will perish in shame." Then Avram lifted his eyes to the heaven and said, "Great God look at this wicked people and judge them."

Nimrod, who had listened passively as Avram spoke, now slowly rose from his throne. "Arrest him!" he cried. Two guards immediately sprang forward. They led Avram to prison and locked him in a cell, where he remained for ten days.

AVRAM IN THE FURNACE

After the ten days had passed, the king gathered all the princes and heads of the provinces and all the wise men and told them, "You have heard what Avram has done and the insolent words he has spoken. Now judge him and sentence him for his deeds." Their verdict was, "Let him be burned alive. Heat the furnace for three days before this criminal is cast inside." Nimrod exclaimed, "Let the sentence be carried out." Avram was brought out in the presence of 900,000 people. Everyone watched and women and children climbed up on towers to see what would happen.

When the astrologers saw Avram they said, "O king, this is the man whom we knew as a child and he was represented by the star which swallowed the other four stars. Did not his father deceive you?"

Nimrod demanded the truth and Terach admitted that he had deceived him. He said, bowing his head, "Forgive me. It was compassion for my son that prevented me from handing him over at birth. Besides, I am really not to blame, for Charan, my oldest son, advised me to deceive the king." (Charan was 32 years old at the time of Avram's birth). This was not true as Terach had acted entirely on his own. When Nimrod heard this, he condemned Charan to the flames as well. Charan, too, was of the same mind as Avram but he concealed his true beliefs out of fear. He thought, "If Avram wins his case, I will declare openly for him. If he loses, I will turn away from him." Both brothers were stripped and bound. God had pity on Avram and an angel descended and delivered him from the furnace. He was unscathed, but the ropes with which his hands and feet were bound were consumed by the fire. He walked about in the fire. His brother, Charan, met a different fate. He perished in the fire and turned to ashes, because he had wavered in his faith in God. Even the soldiers who had cast him into the fire were burned by flames. Avram remained in the furnace for three days.

The king sent men to verify the report that Avram was alive. Still unconvinced, Nimrod came to see the miracle with his own eyes. He was astounded and at once, he ordered, "Take Avram out of the furnace." The men who were sent to the furnace could not approach, as flaming tongues of fire threatened to engulf them. Eight men died in attempting to get Avram out. When Nimrod saw this, he called out, "Come forth Avram, servant of God in heaven, and come to me." When Avram came out with all the cords singed, Nimrod asked him, "Tell me, how have you been rescued?" Avram said, "The God of heaven and earth, in whom I trust and in Whose hand are all things, delivered me from the fire."

Charan was eighty-two years old when he perished in Ur of Kasdim. All the princes who had witnessed Avram's miraculous escape, bowed to Avram. He said, "Do not bow to me, but bow to the God of the world Who made you all. Serve Him and walk in His ways." This impressed the king and all those present. He gave Avram many gifts, among which were his two most important servants. One was called Oni and the other Eliezer. All the princes also gave Avram gifts of gold, silver and precious jewels. Avram departed peacefully and three hundred men who became his followers accompanied him. He returned to his father's house and continued to serve God. He also influenced many people to serve God. Then Avram and his brother Nachor, took wives of the daughters of their brother Charan. The name of Nachor's wife was Milkah and Avram's wife was Sarai. Sarai did not bear children at this time.

Nimrod's Dream

Two years after the deliverance of Avram from the furnace, when he was fifty-two years old, a singular event happened. Nimrod was sitting in his palace in Bavel and he fell asleep. He dreamed that he was standing with his army in a valley opposite the furnace and he saw a man with a drawn sword. This man resembled Avram. The man with the sword was approaching him quickly. The king fled and ran farther and farther away. The same man now threw an egg at the king's head. The egg became a river into which all his army fell and were drowned. The king himself fled with three men who were clothed in royal garments. As they fled, the river became smaller and changed back to the egg, as it was before. From this egg came forth a small bird which pierced the eye of the king. The king became frightened and awoke.

Nimrod was very troubled about this dream, so he sent for Anoki his astrologer. Anoki told the king as follows, "This vision is about Avram and his children who will one day fight against your Majesty. They will defeat your armies. His family will grow and become as mighty as the river you saw. Then you yourself fleeing with three men and the river becoming an egg again and the bird piercing your eye. This tells of one of Avram's offspring who will one day kill you. It is now fifty-two years since your wise men saw that vision in the sky. So long as Avram lives, you will never be safe. Kill him now and rid yourself of this menace."

Nimrod listened carefully to this advice and sent his guards to seize Avram. Eliezer (who had been given to Avram, but happened to be staying at the palace) had overheard Anoki's wicked counsel. He ran at once to inform Avram of the impending danger and reached Avram before Nimrod's men arrived. Avram thus made good his escape to the home of Noach and his son Shem and he hid there. Nimrod's servants searched every place but to no avail. They could not find Avram. When it was clear that Avram would not be found, the king became angry. In time, however, the incident was forgotten.

AVRAM DEPARTS

After living at Noach's house for one month, Avram's father, Terach, came to visit him. Avram said to his father, "Do you not see that I am being sought by the king? Do you not think that it would be safer for all of us to leave this vicinity and go to Canaan? This departure will save our lives. The king shows you favor, but not for your sake. It is only for his own advantage. In any case, all the richness and splendor that you have here is only vanity. So accompany me and we shall then serve God and abandon the emptiness of these surroundings."

Terach saw the wisdom in Avram's advice and acted accordingly. Terach took his son, Avram, and Lot, his grandson, who was the son of Terach's son, Haran, and Sarai, his daughter-in-law, wife of Avram, his son, and all the people of his household. They left Ur in Bavel and made their way to Canaan. They came to the land of Charan and spent three years there as it was a very beautiful and spacious territory.

The people of Charan, upon seeing the goodness of Avram and that God was with him, came and attached themselves to Avram. He taught them God's ways and laws.

AVRAM ENTERS CANAAN

Three years passed, and God appeared to Avram and said, "I am God who brought you out of Ur and saved you from your enemies. Now obey Me and I will make your offspring as numerous as the stars of heaven and I will send My blessing on you. Now, arise, take your wife and all your belongings and go to the Land of Canaan." Avram left for Canaan with his wife and belongings. He was seventy-five years old when he left Charan.

Upon arriving there, Avram pitched his tent among the Canaanites who dwelled in the land. God appeared to him and said, "This is the land which I give to your children for all time and I will make your descendants as numerous as the stars of heaven and I will give to your children all these lands as an inheritance." Avram then built an altar at this place and called upon God's name.

After three years in Canaan, when Avram was seventy-eight years old, Noach died. He had lived nine hundred and fifty years. Avram now settled with his household in Canaan. His father, Terach, and his brother stayed on at Charan.

Five years passed, and the men of Sedom and Amorah and all the cities of the plain rebelled against their overlord, Kedorlaomer, who was the king of Elam. For twelve years they had paid him an annual tribute. In the thirteenth year, however, they rebelled. Nimrod, upon hearing that the people of the plain had rebelled against his former captain, Kedorlaomer, seized the opportunity to go to war against him. When the great dispersion took place after the building of the tower, Kedorlaomer went to Elam and made himself its ruler.

Nimrod met Kedorlaomer in battle in the valley of Bavel. This valley is between Elam and Shinar. All the kings joined in the battle. Nimrod and his army were defeated by the soldiers of Kedorlaomer. Nimrod lost many men and Mardan, son of Nimrod, fell in battle. Nimrod escaped with his life and fled to his own land in great shame and submitted to Kedorlaomer. The latter returned to his own country and sent the captains of his army to the kings in that area — to Aryoch, king of Elasar, to Tidal, king of Goyim — and he made a pact with them.

In the fifteenth year after Avram's arrival in Canaan when Avram was ninety years old, God appeared to him and said, "I am the God Who brought you out of Ur in order to give you this land. Therefore, walk before me and be perfect. To you and your offspring I will give this land to inherit, from the River of Egypt to the River Euphrates. You will join your ancestors in peace in a good old age. The fourth generation will return here and will possess it for all time."

Avram then returned to Charan to visit his father. He stayed there with his household for five years. While in Charan, many men joined Avram and Avram taught them God's instruction. He taught them to know God.

Lech Lecha

Avram's Call and Migration

It happened in those days when Avram was still in Charan, that God appeared to him and said, "Did I not tell you twenty years ago that you must leave your country and birthplace and your father's home and go to the land which I will show you. This land will be given to you and to your children. There I will make you great." He was told to wake up early and leave his place with his wife and all his belongings. He took with him the people who had joined him in Charan and all who were born in his house.

So they left Charan, as God had commanded. Avram also took with him his nephew, Lot, the son of his brother, Haran. Avram was seventy-five years old when he left to go to Canaan. He came to Canaan as God had told him and he pitched his tent on the Plains of Moreh.

Rakyan's Rise to Power

In those days there lived a man in the land of Shinar whose name was Rakyan. He was wise and well-versed in all the sciences and he was very handsome. But he was extremely poor. In desperation Rakyan decided to leave Shinar and travel to Egypt in the hope of being granted an audience at the royal court of Asverus, son of Anam, the King of Egypt. This poor man, Rakyan, expected great things to happen, believing that he would be helped by King Asverus.

Much to his dismay, when he arrived in Egypt he was told by the people whom he met: "It is impossible to see the king at this time. You see, it is our king's custom never to leave his palace, except once a year. At that time he meets with his people and hears everyone's petitions and dispenses justice to all." When Rakyan heard this, he was very disappointed.

One night, as he wandered through the deserted streets, he found shelter in an empty house near a bakery. The aroma of the freshly baked bread made him even more hungry and depressed, so that he could not sleep at all. His future looked very bleak indeed. The next morning, as he walked aimlessly about the streets, he saw vendors of vegetables. He thought about taking up this trade but he was, as yet, unfamiliar with the Egyptian way of life. He bought some produce to open a fruit stand of his own, but before he could sell even one apple he found himself surrounded by a band of ruthless robbers who swiftly grabbed the fruits and vegetables from him. Totally dejected, he returned to the place where he had slept the previous night — brooding over his dismal fate.

Suddenly a thought struck him — truly a brilliant scheme. He got up early in the morning and returned to the place where he was robbed. There, he hired a band of thirty rough and tough outcasts, and led them far into the desert, to the caves where the Egyptians buried their dead. Once there, Rakyan disclosed his plan to the men. He announced: "The king had ordained that no person is to bury his dead unless he pays a fee of two hundred pieces of silver. Henceforth, *we* will enforce this ordinance, and *we* will collect the royal burial tax."

After only eight months, Rakyan and his company of cut-throats had amassed a fortune. Rakyan himself now lived in a palatial estate. He was clothed in fine silks and served by many slaves.

Inevitably, the annual day of the king's public appearance arrived. At long last, the people had the opportunity to lodge their complaint against the new burial tax.

"Oh Majesty," they said, "may you live forever and ever. Forgive us our impertinence, but, pray, tell us, what is the meaning of this exorbitant fee you have imposed on us? Not only do you tax the living — now even the dead are taxed! It is unendurable."

When the king was told what had occurred at the burial caves, he was livid with rage. Rakyan, anticipating the king's fury, had rounded up one thousand children, clothed them in fine embroidered linen, and presented them to the king as slaves. To crown it all, he brought the king magnificent gifts of gold, silver and precious stones. The people were dazzled by the sight of the glittering jewels, and the king was very pleased. The king, smiling benignly, asked Rakyan to tell him the story of his life. Rakyan, a gifted storyteller, kept the king spellbound, stirring his emotions. By the time Rakyan had finished his story, tears were welling from the king's eyes. King Asverus declared: "Rakyan, all is forgiven." In a choked voice he continued, "From this day forward, your name is no longer Rakyan, rather let it be Pharaoh, since you managed to "extract such payment" from the dead. Through intrigue and flattery, Rakyan persuaded the king to appoint him as his second in command.

The new viceroy came out to judge the people daily while the secluded King Asverus continued his practice of appearing in public once a year. By his cunning, Rakyan gradually assumed total rule and levied exorbitant taxes which justified even more his newly acquired title Pharaoh — "the one who made everyone pay." Once his overthrow of King Asverus was complete, Rakyan ascended the throne of Egypt. He eventually established a dynasty, and it was inscribed in the statutes that, henceforth, all kings of Egypt be called by the title of Pharaoh.

Avram in Egypt

There was now a famine in the land of Canaan and the people of that land were impoverished. Avram and his household headed south to Egypt. When they reached the River of Egypt, the caravan rested. As Avram and Sarai walked by that stream he saw the reflection of his wife's face in the water. Noting for the first time that she was truly beautiful, he said to her, "Now that I see that you are so beautiful, I am afraid that the people of this country will kill me in order to take you, as these people do not fear God. So say you are my sister and we shall all be safe." This warning was also issued to all of Avram's people and they were instructed always to refer to Sarai as Avram's sister. As a further precaution, and to guard her from the improper gaze of strangers, Avram hid Sarai in a box.

The caravan then proceeded to the border of Egypt. At their point of entry, they were stopped by customs officers who demanded, "You must pay a tariff of one tenth of the value of your possessions to the ruler." The inspectors noticed the box and, their curiosity aroused, ordered, "Open this box, let us see what is inside." Avram offered a huge sum of money as an alternative to opening the box. This, however, served only to increase their suspicions that the box contained a huge amount of precious stones or the like, and Avram's offer was flatly refused. Pushing Avram aside, they forcibly opened the box, and much to their surprise, they found a woman instead of pearls and rubies. When Sarai emerged from the box they were overwhelmed by her beauty, for no woman of such charm and allure had ever been seen in Egypt. Word of her unequaled grace quickly spread and before long it reached the ears of Pharaoh himself.

Pharaoh sent for her and was so pleased that he rewarded those who had told him about her. Avram was deeply troubled about this and he prayed to God that Sarai be saved from shame. Sarai also prayed, "You, Oh God, told my husband to leave his native land, having promised him many good things. We have done as You commanded. We traveled to Canaan to a people unknown to us. Now we journeyed to a new country, to Egypt, in order to avoid hunger. Now this unhappy event has befallen us. Save us from the evil person who plans to do us harm and do good to us for Your own sake." God heard this prayer and sent His angel to protect her.

Now the king came and sat with Sarai. God's angel quickly told her, "Have no fear, for God has heard your prayer." Then Pharaoh asked her, "What relation are you to the man who brought you here?" She answered, "He is my brother." The king said: "It will be my pleasure to make your brother prominent and prosperous." Thereupon, he sent to Avram gifts of gold and servants along with a request that he appear at the royal court. When Avram came, great honor was bestowed upon him.

In the meantime, whenever the king tried to approach Sarai, he was smitten by the angel with boils and a dreadful skin disease. This occurred time and again. Not only was the king stricken, but all his servants' skin erupted with boils. Great cries and wailing resounded from the palace. Finally, the king understood that his abduction of Sarai was the cause of all this misfortune. Realizing this, he kept away from her and asked her again softly, "Who is that man accompanying you?" Then she admitted saying, "In truth, he is my husband. Please understand that I denied it for fear that he might be hurt on my account."

The angel, aware that Pharaoh repented of the wrong he had committed, refrained from injuring the king and his courtiers. Now that he was healed, the king called Avram and said, "Now take your wife and leave us, before we all perish." He also presented Avram with cattle and sheep and he returned Sarai to him.

Pharaoh so respected Avram that he took a young woman who had been born to him from a concubine and told her, "It will be better for you to become a servant in Avram's house than to remain a princess in the court of Egypt."

So Avram left Egypt and was allowed to depart peacefully with all his belongings and household. He returned to Canaan and went to the place of the altar which he originally had built where he had pitched his tent at the start.

AVRAM AND LOT

Lot, the nephew of Avram, who accompanied him, also had much cattle because God had made him prosperous on his uncle's account. But when Avram returned to Canaan there developed fierce quarrels between the shepherds of his sheep and those of Lot. The land could not support both sets of shepherds and flocks living together. The sheep of Avram were never permitted to pasture on the fields which belonged to other people. This, however, was not the case with Lot's shepherds who did not show any regard for the property of others. It was only natural that people came and complained to Avram about Lot's shepherds. Avram rebuked his nephew, both for the wrong committed against his neighbors and for spoiling the good reputation which Avram had enjoyed among the inhabitants of Canaan. This rebuke was repeated daily, but Lot did not pay heed to his uncle's admonition.

Then Avram said to Lot, "How long will you remain a snare to me and spoil my relations with the people of this land? Let's not have friction between us or between our herdsmen. After all, we're brothers. Why not separate? Choose for yourself the place which you wish to occupy and I shall keep far away from you. But should any harm befall you, let me know, and I promise that I shall come to your aid and defend you."

Lot looked up and saw the entire Jordan plain and was well aware that it was a fertile place, good for man and sheep, as it had excellent pastureland. So he left Avram and pitched his tent in Sedom. Avram, on the other hand, settled in the plains of Mamre, (actually in Chevron), where he remained for many years.

THE WAR OF THE KINGS

It was around this time that Kedorlaomer, King of Elam, sent emissaries to all the kings around him — the king of Shinar — Nimrod, the king of Goyim — Tidal, and Aryoch, the king of Elasar. He had made a treaty with all these and now said, "Come and help me to defeat Sedom and its surrounding cities because they have risen up against me and have remained in rebellion for thirteen years." As soon as these four kings heard Kedorlaomer's call to arms, they came with a mighty force of 800,000 warriors and slew all who came in their path.

All the kings of Sedom and Amorah — five of them — went to battle with the above four. The latter were, Shinav, king of Admah, Shemever of Tzevaim, Bera of Sedom, Birsha of Amorah and Bela of Tsoar. In all, there were nine kings; and nine armies engaged in ferocious combat in the Valley of Siddim. When the dust settled after the battle, the kings of Sedom and Amorah were defeated and fled.

The Valley of Siddim was full of lime pits. The fleeing kings became trapped in these pits, while their troops climbed into the hills to escape. When the allies of the king of Elam reached the gates of Sedom, they took their spoil from that city, turned around and left.

Then Og, the giant, a servant of Avram, came and told his master the distressing news, "Your nephew, Lot, has been taken captive by the victors." Without hesitating, Avram armed his trained men, three hundred eighteen in number. They attacked and pursued these mighty kings throughout the night. When morning dawned, the invincible kings and their powerful armies meekly surrendered to Avram. Only the kings remained alive and each one went his own way. Now Avram brought back the spoils of Sedom, reinstated Lot, and gave him back his captured possessions, which the kings had taken.

On his return, Avram passed through Siddim, and king Bera of Sedom, who had been trapped there, was now able to come forth and greet Avram. Malki-Tzedek, king of Shalem (Jerusalem) also was there and he came to greet Avram, bringing with him bread and wine (a symbol of hospitality and welcome), and they rested at that place, the Valley of the King. Then Malki-Tzedek blessed Avram and Avram gave him a tenth of what was taken from the battle spoil, since Malki-Tzedek was a priest of God. The king of Sedom appealed to Avram, "Give me the captives. You can keep the goods." But Avram said, "I have sworn by the Most High God, who made heaven and earth, that I would not take anything which is yours, nor would I want you to even say, "It was I who made Avram rich." So take what you wish and, as for me, I shall not take anything, from a thread to a shoelace.

Avram did, however, stipulate, "Only what the young soldiers have eaten, should be paid. Oner, Eshkol and Mamre should be given their share." These were his confederates. Not only the soldiers who saw action, but even those who were assigned to stay behind the scene of battle and guard the baggage were to take an equal share with the rest.

The kings of Sedom gave Avram's helpers what had been asked by him. Avram, himself, remained faithful to his word and took nothing. He bade farewell to the kings and their men. His nephew, Lot, was sent away in peace with his possessions which had been restored to him. Lot returned to Sedom and Avram went on his way to the plains of Mamre in Chevron.

BRIS MILAH

At that time, God appeared to Avram and said, "I will make a covenant between Me and you and I will multiply your offspring greatly. This is My covenant. Circumcise all males — you and your children after you — for all time. This shall be performed at the age of eight days so that My covenant will be in their flesh as an everlasting sign. No longer shall your name be Avram but now it will be Avraham, and as to your wife, her name will not be Sarai but Sarah, and I will bless you and multiply your offspring which will become a great nation. Kings will go forth from you."

So Avraham arose and did exactly as he had been commanded. All the men of his household and those whom he had acquired as servants were circumcised, as God had commanded. His son, Yishmael, son of Hagar the Egyptian maidservant, was thirteen years old when his father, Avraham, circumcised him.

On the third day after circumcision, Avraham left his tent and sat at the entrance in order to receive the healing benefit of the sun's warmth.

Vayeira

Three Heavenly Visitors

Now God appeared to Avraham on the Plains of Mamre. Three angels were sent to him in order to visit him in this state of recovery. He was sitting at the entrance of his tent and he raised his eyes and noticed that three men were approaching him. He accordingly rose and greeted them and bowed down. He invited them into his home. He said, "Please do not turn aside. Rather, enter my home and partake of a meal." After urging them, they entered. He placed water before them so that they could wash their feet from the sand. He sat them beneath a tree while he ran and took a young calf and gave it to a servant to prepare for meat. He also told his wife, Sarah, "Hasten and get three measures of fine flour, knead it and bake cakes." She did so. Then Avraham hurried and brought curd and milk to satisfy their hunger until the meat was ready.

When the meal was ended, one of the visitors said to Avraham, "I shall indeed return to you at this time next year when your wife Sarah will have borne a son." Then the angels arose and departed, each in order to fulfill the purpose for which he had been sent.

The Sins of Sedom

In those days, the men of Sedom and Amorah, as well as the entire five cities (these include Admah, Tzevoim and Tso'ar) were extremely wicked and they provoked God by their abominations. They committed such heinous crimes that the cries against these cities rose up before God.

There was a plain in their territory which was so wide that it took half a day to traverse. It contained springs and pastureland. The people of these cities would visit this plain for four days each year. They brought their wives and children with them and they would enjoy themselves with dances and drums beating to the tune of cheerful music. During this time, men would snatch other men's wives and daughters and violate them. Nobody would complain or protest as joyous outings degenerated into wild orgies. This merriment went on day and night and the practice was performed annually. Merchants would come from afar in order to sell their wares but men, women and even children would rob them of their goods. When the merchants complained that nothing was left of all their merchandise, each would say that he had only snatched a small amount not worth talking about, and no claim would be pressed. If the merchant did seek a judge for reparation, the men would throw him out of the place by force.

One day, a man came from Elam. He was riding a donkey on which was a fine, beautifully colored spread. When it became dark, the man had no place to sleep, as no one would let him into their home. He had no choice but to lie down in the street. There was, at that time, a man of Sedom who was as wicked as the rest, and also very cunning. He was given to cruel tricks. The man's name was Chiddud (meaning sharp-whitted). He noticed the stranger in the street and he asked him, "Where do you come from, and where are you headed?" The stranger replied, "I am coming from Chevron; my destination is my home town of Elam. I am spending the night in the streets, for no one has allowed me into his home. He was fortunate in having with him some little food for himself and the donkey. Chiddud asked him to come to his home and promised that he would be comfortable.

He accepted the invitation and in the morning, as he was preparing to leave, Chiddud insisted, "Please, do stay one more day." He stayed on, and the next morning he was determined to leave, but the host again asked him to spend one more day in his home. This time he refused and as he prepared to depart, Chiddud's wife rebuked her all-too-generous husband for being so lavish with his hospitality. Chiddud, with a meaningful wink, told his wife, "Keep quiet, I know what I am doing!" Indeed, he knew only too well.

The stranger took his donkey and asked Chiddud, "Please return to me the decorated spread which I deposited with you for safekeeping." Chiddud said, "What are you talking about?" This is something you must have dreamed. Don't worry, you are in luck, for I am an interpreter of dreams by profession, and I will be glad to interpret your dream for you." He then complimented the poor man, "You certainly had an auspicious dream. The sheet, which is spread, means length and this means that your life will be long. As to the colors, they imply that some day you will also possess a beautiful vineyard." He also told the guest, "I assure you, your dream will come true very soon." The poor man insisted, "Chiddud, believe me, it was no dream." Thereupon, Chiddud coldly informed him, "Locally, people give me four pieces of silver for interpreting dreams, but, since you are my guest, I will only ask for three."

The poor man went to the judge whose name was Serek (anagram of Sheker — falsehood). The judge, stroking his white beard, said, "Chiddud is a man who is known as an interpreter of great accuracy. He is, indeed, much sought after." Chiddud, with such support, now claimed the regular fee of four pieces of silver and full payment for his meals and bed, since the guest was so ungrateful. Close to tears, the man said, "I am willing to pay for the meals and the lodging, but, your honor, I ask that my possessions be returned to me." The judge Serek said, "I am so impressed with Chiddud's interpretation and generous treatment of his guest, I herewith order this ungrateful scoundrel expelled from our city." The men of Sedom saw to it that he was thrown out, without delay.

Sedom and the four cities had four judges. Their names were as follows: Serek, who has just been mentioned (*sheker* — falsehood) was a judge in Sedom. In Amorah, the judge was one "Sharkar" (another form of *sheker*), Zanbach in Admah and Manon in Tzevoim. Eliezer, the servant of Avraham, whom we shall meet soon, gave his own titles to these men. He called Serek, Shikra and he called Sharkar, Shakrura (great liar). Zanbach, he called Kazvan (anagram of Zanbach and meaning liar) and he called Manon, Matzlai Din, a perverter of justice. These judges advised the people to get beds ready and place them in the streets, so that if any wayfarer had the impudence to enter their towns, they would be placed in these beds by force. Three men would hold him by the head and three by the feet. If the man was too short for the bed, they would stretch him mercilessly and if he was too long, they would press him into it. To his howls of anguish they replied, "This is the way we treat all our guests."

From that time on, no person came to Sedom, as it was manifestly clear that they were set against hospitality. Indeed, they would give money to an itinerant beggar but no person was permitted to sell him food, so that he died from starvation and the money was retrieved by the givers. The man was then stripped of his belongings and thrown into a pit in the desert.

One day the good Eliezer visited Sedom in order to see Lot, the nephew of his master, Avraham, and to inquire as to his welfare. When he reached the city, he saw a citizen fighting with some stranger. In the end, the stranger was beaten and stripped of his clothes. Angrily, Eliezer rebuked the attacker. The latter asked Eliezer, "Is he your brother, or are you now a judge in our city?" Eliezer held his own and went so far as to try to get the clothes of the poor man and dress him. In return, Eliezer got a stone thrown at his head by the attacker. Instantly, blood came gushing from the open wound. Seeing the blood, the citizen of Sedom demanded from Eliezer a sum of money as a fee for blood-letting. (Blood-letting was then part of medical treatment.) Eliezer, who refused to pay, went to the judge, Serek, who ruled in favor of the attacker and his claim. Now Eliezer took a stone and flung it at the head of the judge and when blood began to flow he said, "Now, your honor, you must pay me for the medical treatment I administered to you. According to the verdict you just pronounced, you owe me this fee." Eliezer departed and went on his journey.

It happened that when the kings of Elam fought with the kings of Sedom, it was Avraham who had rescued the king of Sedom and his team and the kings brought back spoil from the battle. It was Avraham who had insisted that his nephew, Lot, be given back the possessions which were taken from him by the victors, and the king of Sedom had to submit to that arrangement.

At that time, Lot's wife gave birth to a daughter whose name was Paltis. The girl later married a citizen of Sedom. One day a needy person entered Sedom. As soon as the people learned that he had arrived, they issued a proclamation that it was forbidden to give food to any stranger. But Lot's daughter was goodhearted and compassionate and secretly supplied him with food.

This is how she did it. She would go out to draw water from the well, carrying an empty pitcher on her way which she would fill with food for the poor man. While passing him in his usual place, she would secretly hand him the food. The people of Sedom wondered, "How can a man survive for such a long time without food," since no one was to have given him food. So three men hid themselves at the very spot where the man used to wait. Before long, they saw that it was Paltis who handed him food. They seized her with force and brought her before the judge and she was burned alive as a punishment.

Also in the city of Admah, a neighboring city of Sedom, a girl had given food to a poor man. This man had slept in the street outside this girl's home. When the child opened the door in the morning and saw the disheveled man, she gave him some food. This act angered the men of Admah and the girl was taken to be judged for her crime! She was condemned to death for having broken the rules of the city. They covered her with honey and placed her before a swarm of bees. The bees stung her entire body. The poor girl cried bitterly and no one took notice of her agony. But God saw this act and this sealed the fate of these wicked cities.

Sedom Destroyed

God sent two of the three angels who had visited Avraham to make their way to Sedom. Lot was sitting at the entrance of the city. He arose and greeted them and asked them to dine in his house. But the angel merely urged Lot, "Get out of the city at once. God has sent us to destroy this place." They took hold of Lot, his wife and his daughters and rushed them out of the city, as they screamed, "Get moving! Get out of this area. God is about to destroy the city by fire and brimstone." The whole population, together with the ground's produce will be wiped out. The angel persisted, "Run for your life! Don't look back! Don't stop anywhere in the valley!"

In spite of having been warned by the angel not to look back, Lot's wife, whose name was Lais, was concerned about those daughters who had remained. When she turned to see what was happening to her city she was transformed into a pillar of salt. The oxen used to lick at this salt statue whenever they passed by, but it would grow back again, and the pillar remained as it first was — until today.

Lot and his daughters now took refuge in the cave of Adullam. They stayed there for two days. Indeed, the destruction had been so devastating that Avraham saw the heavy smoke from his abode many miles away.

The daughters of Lot gave their father wine in order to get him intoxicated. They believed that the whole world had been destroyed and that they were the last inhabitants. They wished that the human race could be preserved through their children. The son of the older daughter was named Moav (meaning *Me'av* — from my father) and the younger daughter's son was called Ben Ammi (son of my people). These were the ancestors of the nations of Ammon and Moav. They left the cave and settled in another place across the Jordan River and their offspring became very numerous.

SARAH AND AVIMELECH

While journeying from the region of Mamre in order to go to the land of the Philistines Avraham stopped at the city of Gerar. This happened twenty-five years after he settled in the land of

Canaan. He was now in his hundredth year. Before he reached Gerar, he again told his wife, "When anyone asks you about me, always tell them that I am your brother." He did this in order to spare them both the ordeal which they had endured in Egypt, and which was explained in the story of the previous *parsha.*

He had not been long in the land when the Philistines were struck by Sarah's great beauty. They asked about the relationship and they were told that Avraham was Sarah's brother. Then some men reported the matter to their king, Avimelech. They said, "A man just arrived here and he has brought with him a very beautiful woman who is his sister."

Avimelech took note of this report and sent for Sarah. He was very pleased with her and asked her, "Who is the man with whom you are traveling?" "He is my brother," she replied. The king then made the following offer to Avraham, "My whole country is open to you. You may settle wherever you see fit; moreover, I will appoint you to a very high office in my government. Indeed, Avraham was shown great honor by all.

That evening, as it became dark, the king fell asleep while sitting on his throne and did not awake until morning. During that sleep he had a frightening dream. In it he saw an angel fast approaching him with a drawn sword, as if to kill him.

Avimelech cried, "What sin have I committed that you wish to kill me?"

The angel said, "You are about to perish because of the woman who was brought to you yesterday, since she is a married woman. She is the wife of Avraham. Restore her at once to her husband before you and all your court perish."

Indeed, during that night there was a great cry in the whole Philistine region. During this short period of time, no woman was able to give birth to a child, and all the bodily functions of men and women had come to a halt.

That morning, Avimelech arose trembling. He sent for all his servants and told them about his dream. They advised him, "Return this woman to her husband, for if you don't, you will suffer the same fate as Pharaoh in Egypt who was afflicted with boils and rashes for abducting her." Sarah was swiftly returned to Avraham and Avimelech was most anxious to avert further suffering to himself and his land.

Now Avimelech summoned Sarah and Avraham to his palace, where he asked Avraham, "Why did you not tell me that she is your wife?" Avraham answered, "I realized that there is no fear of God in this place. I was afraid that I might be killed because of my wife. The king now presented Avraham with cattle and servants and gave him one thousand pieces of silver. Avimelech said, "Here, my land is before you and you may dwell in any part of it which pleases you."

Avraham now took up his abode in Gerar. As the servants of the king were still suffering, the king asked Avraham, "Please pray for them and ask that their sufferings end." Avraham prayed to God for Avimelech and his people and his prayers were accepted, so that they were again able to bear children.

YITZCHAK AND YISHMAEL

At that time, just after Avraham had settled in the land of the Philistines, God was mindful of Sarah and she gave birth to a son. He was called Yitzchak. Avraham circumcised his son at the age of eight days. Avraham was then one hundred years old. When his son was weaned, Avraham made a great feast. This banquet was attended by Shem and Ever and all the great men of that time. Avimelech, king of Gerar, and his chief captain, Pichol, attended. Terach, the father of Avraham, and Avraham's brother, Nachor, also came from far-away Charan to join in his happiness. It was just then that Serug, son of Reu died. This was when Yitzchak was one year old. Serug had lived for two hundred and thirty-nine years. Yishmael, the son of Avraham, was a lad of fourteen years, when Yitzchak was born. He had become an expert archer. When Yitzchak was five years old, Yishmael was sitting at the door of his tent. Suddenly he drew his bow and aimed it at Yitzchak. Sarah saw this and she tore the bow away from Yishmael just in time. Sarah now insisted, "Drive away this maid-servant, Hagar, together with her son. The son of this slave will not share the inheritance with my son, Yitzchak." She told Avraham about Yishmael's intention to kill Yitzchak.

Avraham listened to his wife and got up early the next morning and took twelve loaves of bread and a container of water and gave these to Hagar and sent her away. Hagar and her son went toward the desert and lived in the wilderness of Paran. Before returning to Egypt, where she had been born, Hagar arranged for her son, Yishmael, to marry Merivah. Merivah had four sons and one daughter. Together with her husband, Yishmael, they set up their tents in the wilderness and moved about as nomads. Each month they would dismantle their tents and move elsewhere, but they never visited Avraham.

YISHMAEL'S WIVES

Now after a time, Avraham said to Sarah, "I must visit Yishmael, since I long to see him again." He saddled his camel and journeyed, having heard about the place where Yishmael and his family were living. After an arduous journey, he arrived and appeared at the tent of Yishmael. Yishmael was not at home, since he had gone hunting. Avraham had promised Sarah that he would not descend from the camel into Yishmael's abode. He did, however, ask, "Please give me a little water, for I am very weary from the long journey." Merivah said, "I can't give you anything. I have neither bread nor water." She left the visitor without even asking him who he was.

Avraham overheard this woman shouting at the children and beating them and she also cursed her husband, Yishmael, in his absence. This annoyed Avraham and he asked her only to come out of the tent and take a message for her husband. "Tell your husband," he said, "that an elderly man was here and describe me to him, and that I come from the land of the Philistines." Tell him as follows, "The very first thing you must do upon your arrival, Yishmael, is to remove the main tent support-beam and replace it with a new one." Then Avraham departed.

When Yishmael returned from his hunt, Merivah told him all that had happened and gave him the message as she had been told. Yishmael listened eagerly and knew that the visitor was his father. From her account, he understood that his wife had not shown him respect. He also understood the meaning of Avraham's short message and he divorced this wife and took another.

Three years later, Avraham again longed to see his son, Yishmael. Again he arrived at noontime. His son's wife came from the tent and said, "He is not here, sir, as he went to hunt but please come in, as you must be weary and hungry." Avraham said, "I cannot stay, I must continue on my way, but I would be happy to drink some water." The woman hastened and brought him bread and water. Avraham uttered blessings on his son Yishmael and blessed God after eating. He told this wife of his son to give her husband a message on his return. "Tell him that the tent's main support-beam is very good and that he must never remove it." When Yishmael returned, his wife told him about this visit and he again understood that this man was his father. He also understood the meaning of his father's cryptic message. Yishmael then blessed God.

Then Yishmael took his wife and children and traveled to the land of the Philistines to join his father, Avraham. Yishmael remained with his father for a long period of time.

AVRAHAM'S WELL

Avraham lived in the land of the Philistines for twenty-six years. He then moved to Chevron where he dug wells of water and remained near these wells. Avimelech, the king, heard that

Avraham had dug a well near the border of his land. His men came and quarreled with the servants of Avraham and robbed him of the well. When Avimelech heard about this, he came with Pichol, the captain of his army and with other men and discussed the matter with Avraham. Avraham rebuked the king for the robbery of the well. Avimelech swore by the Creator of the earth, "I don't know who could have done such a thing. I had no knowledge of it." Avimelech took seven sheep and gave them to Avraham as symbolic evidence that Avraham had indeed dug the well. The king took the seven lambs and swore that he had not heard about the incident. This place was then called Beer Sheva ("well of the oath"). Avimelech then returned to his land.

Avraham's Tent

Avraham settled in Beer Sheva where he planted a tamarisk tree. In his tent he had four entrances, corresponding to the four points of the compass, so that any visitor could enter from the direction of his arrival without delay. The visitor would then receive generous hospitality. If any visitor came hungry, he was fed; if he came dressed shabbily, he was clothed. Avraham's tents stretched as far as Chevron.

Nachor, Avraham's brother, now settled in Charan with his father, Terach. Nachor had sons borne to him by his wife, Milkah, the daughter of Haran. Milkah was Sarah's sister.

These are the names of the sons of Nachor: Utz, Buz, Kemuel, Kesed, Chazo, Pildash, Yidlaf and Besuel — eight sons in all. Nachor had a concubine named Reumah and she bore to him Tevach, Gacham, Tachash and Maachah. So Nachor had in all twelve sons and some daughters too. The sons of Utz were Avicheref, Gadin, Milom, and a daughter, Devorah.

The sons of Buz were Berachel, Naamas, Shuach and Medani. The sons of Kemuel were Aram and Rechov. The sons of Kesed were Anmelech, Mishor, Bagun and Yifi. The sons of Chazo were

Pildash, Mini and Efer. The sons of Pildash were Arod, Amoram, Marid and Melach. The sons of Yidlaf were Moshan, Kushan and Motzi. The sons of Besuel were Sachar and Lavan and a daughter was borne to him named Rivkah.

Aram, son of Kemuel, went with Rechov, his brother, and came upon a plain near the River Euphrates. They built a city there called Pesor which is in the region of Mesopotamia. The sons of Kesed also built a city called Kesed, which was later known as Kasdim.

Terach, Avraham's father, took a wife in his later years and her name was Pelilah. She bore him a son named Tzova, and Terach lived twenty-five years after this event. He died when Yitzchak was thirty-five years old. Terach had lived two hundred and five years.

Tzova, son of Terach, was thirty years old when his son, Aram was born. He also had sons, Akalyo and Marik. Tzova had three wives and had twelve sons and three daughters. God had given Tzova great wealth and he was very prosperous. Tzova left Charan and wandered about, as he could not live in the same area as the sons of Nachor. Eventually, he settled in a land in the east. This territory which he now built up was eventually called Aram Tzova (Allepo) and this is its name to this very day.

PRELUDE TO THE AKEIDAH

Yitzchak, Avraham's son, became very great in those days and his father taught him the ways of God and God was with him. Then one day his brother, Yishmael, taunted him saying, "I was thirteen years old when God commanded my father to circumcise us. I willingly submitted to this painful operation. I did this in obedience to my father and to God. Yitzchak answered, "Why do you boast about sacrificing a small piece of flesh — that is no reason for pride!" He added, "I swear that if God commanded my father to sacrifice me, I would comply joyfully." God heard

Yitzchak's remark and took note of it. He would one day test Avraham by just such a command.

One day the angels came to minister to God and Satan was among them. He was there with the intention of accusing mankind before their Maker.

God said to Satan, "Where have you come from now?" Satan replied, "I have returned from going about the world and searching there." Then God asked, "What can you tell me about the actions of man?" Satan replied, "I see only one thing about mankind and that is that they seek God only when they stand in need of Him, but once they are granted their request, they forget about God." He added, "See what Avraham, son of Terach, did. He had no sons for a long time and he built altars to please You. Once his request for children was granted, he made a great banquet and was full of joy. He has since forgotten You. He killed so many cattle for this feast, but did not offer You an ox or a sheep or even a goat! Now thirty-seven years have passed since this event and he has not offered You one sacrifice."

God replied to Satan as follows, "You have not thought well of My servant, Avraham, since there is no person on earth like him. He is perfect and upright. I am certain that if I were to ask him to sacrifice his only son to Me, he would not refuse. He certainly would be willing to give me his cattle if required." Satan replied, "Very well then, if you so command him I am sure he will not comply."

Avraham is Tested

So God said to Avraham, "Avraham" and he replied, "Here I am." God continued, "Now take your son, your only son, whom you love, Yitzchak, and go to the land of Moriah and offer him up on one of the mountains which I shall show you. You will recognize this mountain by a cloud and the Glory of God over it." Avraham thought, "How can I do this, since I must take him from his mother, Sarah, and then offer him up?" So Avraham came to his wife and gently said to her, "Our son is now a man, but he has not yet learned the ways of God and how to serve Him, so we will go to the house of Shem and his son, Ever. There he will learn all about Godly worship. Sarah agreed to the plan on one condition. "Just do not take him too far away from me and let him not stay away too long, for I am very attached to him."

Sarah's Farewell

Avraham said to his wife, "Please, pray to God that He deals kindly with all of us." So Sarah took Yitzchak and spent the night talking to him, pouring out her heart to him. In the morning she gave her husband instructions about Yitzchak. "My husband," she said crying, "I have no other child. Do not allow him to be hungry and let him not walk barefoot, nor sit in the sun, nor travel unescorted. Indeed, give into all his wishes." She was unable to continue, as she broke into plaintive sobs.

Thereupon, Sarah took one of the best garments, which King Avimelech had given her, and she clothed Yitzchak in it and placed a hat with a precious jewel in it on his head. She gave them food for their journey and escorted them part of the way, until Avraham told her to return home. Sarah sighed, "Who knows whether I shall ever look upon you again?" Upon hearing these words, Avraham and Yitzchak dissolved in tears. Sarah was accompanied by servants who wished to bid farewell also, and when Avraham told them to return, they left after much weeping.

Yishmael and Eliezer

Avraham took his two lads with him; Yishmael, the son of Hagar, and Eliezer, Avraham's servant. They were to accompany him on the entire journey. While traveling, Yishmael and Eliezer held a heated conversation.

Yishmael began, "I know that my father is planning to offer Yitzchak as a sacrifice to God. When he will return alone, I will be his only heir, and I will inherit all his possessions. After all, I am his first-born."

Eliezer replied, "Your father once drove you out of his house, together with your mother, and he said that he would never make you his heir. So to whom will he leave his possessions if not to me, his faithful servant? I have served him faithfully day and night and when he dies, he will leave everything to me." They argued heatedly for many hours.

Satan Appears

As Avraham traveled with Yitzchak, Satan appeared in the guise of a very gentle and humble old man. He approached Avraham and said, "Are you such a fool, so stupid as to carry out the thing you are planning to do? He is your only child, given to you in your old age and, for no reason, you are now going to destroy him. How can this be God's will? God would not ask of anyone to sacrifice his son!" Avraham knew that this was Satan trying to lead him astray and he ignored him.

Satan was not to be put off and he resorted to another trick. This time he appeared to Yitzchak in the form of a good looking young man. He said to him, "Your father is old and does not know what he is doing and he plans to kill you soon, offering you on the altar. Do not obey him and do not let him deprive the world of such a fine person as yourself."

When Yitzchak heard this, he asked his father, "Father, have you heard what this stranger told me?" Avraham answered, "Pay no attention to this talk, since it is Satan who wishes to deter us from obeying God's orders."

Avraham rebuked Satan and when the latter saw that his talking was of no avail, he resorted to a different plan. He transformed himself into a brook, through which Avraham and Yitzchak had to pass while crossing it, the water reached their necks and they became deeply distressed. Avraham knew the area well from his travels, but he had never noticed a brook in this place. He knew, therefore, that this was Satan's work. He again rebuked Satan and added, "God rebuke you Satan!" He told Satan to depart, as this Evil One was obstructing them in the performance of God's will. Satan trembled at the rebuke of Avraham and the water dried up.

THE AKEIDAH

During this three-day journey, Avraham watched for the place which God had chosen for this act of devotion. Then, from a distance, he saw a pillar of fire from the earth to heaven and then a heavy cloud radiating the Glory of God on the mountain. Avraham asked Yitzchak whether he, too, saw this and Yitzchak described the scene exactly as Avraham had seen it. But, when he asked Yishmael and Eliezer about it, they told him, "We have seen nothing unusual. It is a mountain like any other mountain." Then Avraham knew that it was not God's wish that these two proceed with him. He said to them, "Remain here with the donkey, I shall go with Yitzchak and we shall return to you." So they both remained there.

Avraham had taken with him wood which he placed upon Yitzchak's back and he had taken fire and a knife. They both walked on, when Yitzchak said to his father, "I see the fire and wood, but I do not see a lamb for the offering!" Avraham replied, "Son, God had chosen you to be an offering to him." Yitzchak said, "I will do whatever God has commanded and I will do so willingly." When his father asked him whether he had any improper or resentful thoughts about this, Yitzchak answered, "I swear that I turn neither to the right nor to the left and that there is no improper thought in my mind and that no part of my body is afraid. I rejoice that I have been chosen for this act."

Avraham was pleased with the reply and they arrived at the very place which had been designated for the offering. Yitzchak assisted his father in the building of the altar and handed him the stones. Avraham took the wood and arranged it on the altar and he bound Yitzchak. Yitzchak said, "Bind me securely, so that I will not move when the knife touches me and cause the offering to be invalid." He continued, "After I have been killed, take some of the ashes to my mother and tell her that I was accepted as a sacrifice. Do not tell her this while she is sitting near a well or on a high place, since the shock might cause her to fall." Avraham wept on hearing such words and the tears fell on his son. Yitzchak, too, wept as he asked his father, "Do not delay the command of God."

Avraham was now ready to lift the knife when angels of mercy addressed God and asked Him, "Find a substitute for Yitzchak, both father and son have shown their complete willingness to perform Your will." God intervened and told Avraham, "Do not put forth your hand to the lad, nor do anything to harm him. Now I know that you are a Godfearing man and that you would not even withhold your son from me."

Avraham raised his eyes and saw a ram which had been caught in a thicket by its horns. This ram had been created when God made the earth, for the sole purpose of being at the scene of the binding of Yitzchak at this specific moment when it would be needed. The ram was ready to come of its own accord, since it was created for this purpose. Avraham released his son and soon replaced him by this ram whose blood was sprinkled on the alter. Avraham called out in a loud voice, "Let this ram be instead of my son, let its blood be reckoned as my son's blood." God blessed Avraham and his descendants after him.

Satan Deceives Sarah

But Satan had not ended his evil work. He now appeared to Sarah again in the guise of an old and kind man. While Avraham was about to sacrifice his son and Satan had failed in his wiles (both with father and son), he came to Sarah and said, "Do you know what your husband has done? He has built an altar and Yitzchak, your son, appealed to him to desist, but he had no pity on his son." She thought that this man had been asked by Yitzchak to save him. She wept and put ashes on her head. She said, "I would have gladly taken your place this day, my son, whom I reared with such love. My consolation is my knowledge that you fulfilled God's desire. I am proud of what you, dear Yitzchak, have done. But I am torn between pride and sorrow." She placed her head on one of her maidservants and she was as silent as a stone. She arose and went to Chevron and asked all the passers-by, "Has anyone seen my husband and my son?" They were nowhere to be found.

Now Satan appeared to Sarah once more and admitted that he had told her lies, and that Yitzchak had not been killed. She was very happy. This joyful news was too startling for her frail heart and in extreme ecstasy, her soul departed from her and she died. When Avraham ended his task with Yitzchak, he took Yishmael and Eliezer and proceeded home, to Be'er Sheva. They looked for Sarah, but they were told that she had gone to Chevron to seek them, after what she had been told by the stranger.

Avraham and Yitzchak went to Chevron and discovered that Sarah had died. Yitzchak cried out, "My mother, why have you now left me?" Avraham and Yitzchak mourned for Sarah and wept. All the servants mourned deeply. So Avraham and Yitzchak and all the household expressed sorrow at the passing of Sarah.

Chayei Sarah

SARAH'S DEATH

Sarah had lived for one hundred and twenty-seven years and died in Kiryas Arba, which is Chevron in the land of Canaan. After having mourned over his wife, Avraham arose to arrange for his wife's burial. He went to his neighbors, the Chittites, who at that time, inhabited the land. "I am a stranger and a settler among you. Grant me land for a burial place, so that I might give my dead proper burial."

The Chittites answered Avraham, "The land is before you. You may have the best place we have to offer." Avraham then said, "Kindly hear me and entreat Ephron, son of Tzochar, on my behalf, that he will let me have the cave of Machpelah at the far end of this land and I shall purchase this piece of land at the full price."

Ephron was sitting among the others and they summoned him to talk to Avraham. Ephron told Avraham that whatever he wished to have would be his, but Avraham insisted on paying rather than accepting this as a gift. He wished to possess this land for all time as a family plot. Then Ephron said that both the field and the cave would be Avraham's and that Avraham could pay what he thought was enough. But Avraham wished to pay the full price, since he wished it to be his and that no person might ever claim it from him. So Ephron and all his relatives yielded to Avraham's request and the field with the cave was sold for four hundred shekels of silver, and the money was weighed in the presence of the assembly.

Avraham duly recorded the sale in written form, having it signed by four witnesses, whose names were: Amigal, son of Avishua the Chittite; Elchoron, son of Ashunash the Chittite; Avdon, son of Achira the Gamrite and Akdil, son of Abudash the Tzidonite. Then Avraham took the deed of sale and put it in his treasury, having written the following in the document:

> The cave and the field of Machpelah did Avraham buy from Ephron, the Chittite, and from the latter's descendants, and that it now becomes the legal possession of Avraham and of Avraham's descendants as a burial plot to be theirs for all time.

Avraham then buried his wife, Sarah, in that same place with great honor, such as befitting royalty. A number of great men followed the bier, such as: Shem, son of Noach, and the latter's son, Ever. Avimelech, Aner, Eshkol and Mamre. All the important men of the time were present. The period of mourning lasted seven days during which the inhabitants of the country came to console Avraham and Yitzchak.

When the mourning period ended, Avraham sent his son, Yitzchak, to study at the Yeshivah of Shem and Ever. He was to occupy his time in studying the ways of God, and spend three years at this academy. Then Avraham and his household returned to Be'er Sheva to their own homes.

Avimelech, king of the Philistines, died in that year at the age of one hundred ninety-three years and Avraham went with his men to that land to console the family. The men of Gerar took Benmelech, the son of Avimelech, and made him king when he was twelve years old. They now called him Avimelech, as his father had been named, and this remained the custom for all time in Gerar that the king's name was to be Avimelech. The new king began his reign in the thirty-ninth year of the life of Yitzchak.

Lot died at the age of one hundred forty-two. His descendants were Moav and Ben Ammi and the manner of their birth has been told in the previous *sidra,* Vayera. They took wives from the land of Canaan and they had sons. The sons of Moav were Er, Maayon, Tersiyon and Kanvil; four in all. The sons of Ben Ammi were Gerim, Ishon, Rabbos, Tzillon, Einan and Miyon; six in all. These went and established their homes wherever they desired. They became extremely abundant, and, having built cities in the land, named these cities after their own names.

Nachor, Terach's son, Avraham's brother, died at that time in the fortieth year of the life of Yitzchak. He had lived one hundred seventy-two years. He died in Charan and was buried there and was mourned by his brother Avraham for a long time.

A Wife for Yitzchak

Avraham now summoned his chief servant, Eliezer, the overseer of his household. Avraham said, "I am now old and I do not know when I may die, so arise and take a wife for my son, Yitzchak. Go to my own country, to Charan, and I shall bind you by oath by the God Who created heaven and earth that you do not take a wife from the daughters of Canaan for my son." Then the servant asked, "What would happen if the woman would not be willing to follow him and return with him?" Avraham warned him, "Beware, do not take Yitzchak back to his native land, Charan. The God of heaven, Who has taken me from my father's home and Who has promised me that the land of Canaan would be given to me, would also send His angel before the servant and help him."

Then the servant swore that he would follow Avraham's instructions and that he would see to the matter. Eliezer took with him ten men from his master's servants along with the necessary camels. They arose and went to Charan to the city of Nachor. As they were about to depart, Avraham sent for Yitzchak at the home of Shem and Ever and asked that he return home to his father at Be'er Sheva.

Eliezer and his men arrived at Charan — the city of Nachor. They camped near the watering place where each evening the young women used to come to draw water from the wells. Eliezer then prayed, "God of my master, Avraham, grant me good fortune this day and do kindness with my master, Avraham. I stand here by the spring and when I say to a girl, 'Lower your pitcher so that I may drink' and if she answers, 'Drink, and I will give your camels to drink, too,' this shall be the girl who you intend for your servant, Yitzchak."

God heard Eliezer's prayer and it so happened that at that moment, Rivkah, daughter of Besuel, son of Milkah, who was the wife of Avraham's brother, Nachor, came to the well. She was very beautiful and everything happened just as Eliezer had prayed. Eliezer asked her for some water from the pitcher and, after giving him water, she also went to draw more water for the camels. Eliezer then took a gold nose ring and two bracelets and gave them to her and asked her who she was and whether there would be place in her father's home for them to stay the night. She told him that she was the daughter of Besuel, who was the son of Nachor and Milkah, and that there was straw and fodder for the animals and ample place for the men to spend the night. Eliezer was happy and bowed to God.

The girl ran into the house and told her mother and the rest of the family what had happened. She had a brother called Lavan who, having seen the gifts which his sister had with her, now ran out to greet the men and invited them into the house. After they entered Besuel's house, Eliezer disclosed the nature of his errand and how he had prayed for this to happen, as indeed it all did happen. They agreed to allow Rivkah to be Yitzchak's wife after having first asked for, and receiving, her consent. That night, Besuel together with his sons, Lavan and Sachar, made a feast at which they all ate and drank and were very happy. Although they had wished Rivkah to stay on in Charan for some time Eliezer asked them not to detain them.

They left with the blessings of the family. Rivkah was accompanied by her nurse, Devorah, the daughter of Utz. They were given gifts of gold and silver and they returned to Canaan. Yitzchak took Rivkah to his mother's tent, once she had become his wife. He was at that time forty years old.

Then Avraham took another wife from the land of Canaan. Her name was Keturah. She gave birth to Zimron, Yokshan, Medan, Midian, Yishbak and Shuach; six sons in all. The sons of Zimron were Avichen, Molid and Mariah. The sons of Yokshan were Sheva and Dedan. The sons of Medan were Amida, Yov, Gochi, Elisha and Notha. The sons of Midian were Epha, Epher, Chanoch, Avida and Elda'ah. The sons of Yishbak were Machiri, Bidua and Tator. The sons of Shuach were Bildad, Chemdad, Moshana and Mivan. Avraham gave them gifts and sent them away to settle in various places. They went to the Mount of the East and built six cities and remained there. But the sons of Sheva, Dedan and Yokshan, together with their sons did not remain in these cities, but went about in the wilderness as nomads.

The sons of Midian went east to the land of Kush and discovered there a wide plain and built up the region known as Midian. Midian remained there with his five sons.

YISHMAEL

These are the families of Yishmael, son of Avraham, born from Hagar. Yishmael had taken a wife from Egypt and her name was Merivah. The latter gave birth to Nevayos, Kedar, Adbeal, Mivsam and one daughter, Bosmas. Yishmael divorced Merivah, as she was not pleasant in her ways. Then Yishmael took his family and went to Canaan to his father.

Then Yishmael married Malkis who had sons, Mishma, Duma, Massa, Hadad, Tema, Yetur, Naphish and Kedmah. These were the twelve princes of Yishmael whose family spread over a large territory. They went as far as the wilderness of Paran from Chavila to near Assyria.

Yitzchak's wife, Rivkah, was barren in those days. Yitzchak lived with his father, Avraham, in Canaan, God was with him, as he had been with his father.

Arpachshad, son of Shem, died at that time when Yitzchak was forty-eight years old. Arpachshad had lived four hundred and thirty-eight years.

Toldos

Yaakov and Eisav

In the fifty-ninth year of Yitzchak's life, Rivkah, his wife, was still without child. She said to her husband, "I have heard that your mother, too, was childless until your father, Avraham, prayed for her. So stand and beg God on my behalf, too, and He will, for His mercy's sake, hear you too." Yitzchak replied, "My father had already prayed that his descendants multiply and this promise was made concerning me. It can only be that the cause of childlessness is in you." But even so, Rivkah insisted that her husband pray.

Yitzchak listened to his wife and they both went to Mount Moriah to seek God. They came to the place where Yitzchak had offered himself as a sacrifice and there they sought God and prayed to Him. Yitzchak prayed for his wife, "God of heaven and earth, Whose goodness fills the whole world. You took my father from his native land and brought him to this land telling him that You would give his descendants this country and that they would be as numerous as the stars and as the sand of the sea. Let Your word now come true and give us male children. Our eyes and hope are bent on You alone."

God heard his prayer and Rivkah conceived twins. After seven months, the children pressed hard against each other within her body and she was in great distress and pain. She asked the women around her about this and whether anyone had ever experienced such pain. They told her that such had never happened and she asked, "If this is how it is with me, what can it mean?" She went again to Mount Moriah to seek God's guidance. She also traveled to Shem and Ever in search of advice about this strange condition. She also asked her father-in-law, Avraham, to discover by prayer what had occurred in her case. They all replied, "Two children are in your womb from which two nations will arise. One shall be stronger than the other, and the older shall be servant to the younger."

Rivkah finally gave birth to twins. The first one came forth — red all over — like a hair-cloak and this son was called Eisav. The other child came out immediately with his hand grasping the heel of Eisav. They called him Yaakov. Yitzchak was sixty years old when his sons were born.

Eisav grew to be a man of subtle and wily thoughts, knowing the skills of hunting; a man of the open plains and fields. Whereas Yaakov was a settled man who remained in the tents, tending sheep and following the ways of God and the commands of his parents. Yitzchak and his family stayed on with his father, Avraham, in the land of Canaan and Yishmael went to Chavilah. The sons of Avraham's concubines had gone to the east country, having been granted gifts by Avraham.

Avraham gave his best possessions to Yitzchak and charged him as follows: "Do you not know that the God of heaven and earth is the only one Who took me out of my father's house and rescued me from the Kasdim and from the plans of the wicked. I trust Him. He brought me here and promised to give this land to my children if they will obey His precepts and not turn from the correct path. He will protect us from our enemies as long as we remain faithful to Him."

Yitzchak answered, "Whatever my father commands, we shall do." Avraham then blessed Yitzchak and his children and continued teaching Yaakov the ways of God. Avraham died at a ripe old age and was buried by Yitzchak and Yishmael, his sons. When the news of Avraham's death spread, the kings and princes of the land came to do him honor. People journeyed from his native place, Charan — Avraham's family, and also the sons of the concubines. They all came to show kindness to Yitzchak and to console him. Avraham was buried in the cave of Machpelah, which he had brought from Ephron the Chittite.

The inhabitants of the land mourned Avraham for a whole year. He had been good to all men and upright with God. Women and children mourned him too. He had been good from his youth until the day he died and he had been saved from Nimrod and had fought the four kings of Eilam.

He had brought everyone to the service of God and taught the people this service. He had planted the Eishel (tamarisk) and a vineyard and had given all people hospitality in his own tents. God protected the whole land on account of Avraham. When he died, God gave his son, Yitzchak, the same blessing as his father had been given, and he, too, observed the commandments of God. Avraham lived one hundred and seventy-five years.

EISAV SLAYS NIMROD

After Avraham died, Eisav went out to continue his hunting in the open fields and to bring home the catch. Nimrod, king of Bavel, also went on one of his hunting expeditions and was escorted by a great number of his warriors. Nimrod kept a jealous eye on Eisav, since there had been a bitter feud between Nimrod and Eisav.

Nimrod's warriors had wandered off and Nimrod was left with only two men. Eisav now hid in ambush awaiting Nimrod. Nimrod, in search of the other men, had come to the very place where Eisav was waiting. Eisav rushed up with sudden force and with sword in hand killed Nimrod and cut off his head. Nimrod's two companions now attacked Eisav. With lightning-like thrusts, Eisav overpowered both of them and pierced their hearts. The others heard the tumult and the cries, but when they arrived, they found that Nimrod and his two men were dead. Meanwhile, Eisav had taken Nimrod's coat. This was the coat given to him by his father, Kush, and through the power of this coat he had ruled on earth. This was the very coat of Adam and Chavah.

EISAV SELLS HIS BIRTHRIGHT

Eisav then returned home exhausted and in despair and seated himself near his brother, Yaakov. He said, "I am about to perish, to what avail is my birthright." Yaakov acted with care and Eisav sold Yaakov the birthright for red broth which Yaakov had been cooking. He also sold Yaakov his place in the cave of Machpelah for which Yaakov paid. The details were recorded and signed by witnesses and the records were duly kept by Yaakov.

Thus Nimrod, the son of Kush, died and was taken back to Bavel for burial. He had lived two hundred fifteen years and had reigned over all men of the earth for one hundred eighty-five years. But he perished at the hand of Eisav in disgrace. Eisav was the grandson of Avraham and one must recall the dream which Nimrod had that he would be killed by a descendant of Avraham, and now it had come true.

When Nimrod died, his kingdom was divided into many parts among the other kings. Nimrod's servants now became vassals to other kings.

After Avraham died, a great famine was brought by God upon the land. Yitzchak decided to leave to Egypt, as his father had done in similar circumstances. Then God appeared to Yitzchak and said, "Do not go down to Egypt, but go to Gerar to Avimelech, king of that place, and stay there until the famine is over."

Yitzchak journeyed to Gerar where the people of that place noticed that his wife, Rivkah, was very beautiful. Yitzchak had told them that she was his sister, taking the same precautions which his father had taken in Egypt and in Gerar. He was afraid that if they knew she was his wife, they would kill him.

YITZCHAK IN GERAR

After three months, Avimelech happened to glance through the window of his room and he saw Yitzchak sporting with his wife. Yitzchak's home being directly opposite the king's palace. Avimelech summoned Yitzchak and said to him, "What have you done to us. One of the people or nobility might have been intimate with your wife and you would have rendered us liable to guilt."

Yitzchak then explained the reason for his statement that Rivkah was his sister.

Avimelech now issued orders to all the princes and nobles and they brought Yitzchak and his wife before the king, having first dressed them in royal apparel. They were driven through the streets of the city and the following royal proclamation was made. "Whoever touches this man or his wife will be put to death." Then they returned to the palace and God was with Yitzchak, who became great and lacked nothing. The king dealt favorably with Yitzchak and he remembered the treaty which was made between his father and Avraham. Avimelech invited Yitzchak to dwell wherever he wished and make his home in any part of his realm until such time as he wished to return to his own place. Yitzchak was given fields and vineyards and land to sow. He sowed and reaped and ate of the fruit of the land until the famine was over. Yitzchak sowed during that year and reaped a hundred-fold, as God had blessed him.

So Yitzchak became rich. He had sheep and herds and many servants. The famine was over and God appeared to Yitzchak and told him to leave Gerar and to return home to Canaan. He departed for Chevron with his household.

Then Shelach, son of Arpachshad, died at the age of four hundred and thirty-three. Yitzchak sent his younger son, Yaakov, to Shem and Ever to study the ways of God. He was to stay there for thirty-two years. Eisav did not go with Yaakov, as he was not willing to spend time there and was intent on hunting. He became an expert in this activity and also trapped the minds of men by his wiles.

One day Eisav went to hunt in the region of the field of Seir and the field of Edom. He stayed there for four months. There he saw the daughter of a Canaanite man called Be'eri. This man was really the son of Eipher, the Hittite, of the families of Cheis, who was the son of Canaan. The name of this woman was Yehudis and Eisav married her when he was forty years old.

This was a bitter grief to Yitzchak and Rivkah. Eisav brought Yehudis to Chevron, where his parents had settled and he stayed there for some time.

Then Shem, son of Noach, died in the hundred and tenth year of Yitzchak's life, when Yaakov was fifty years old. Shem was six hundred years old when he died. When Yaakov was fifty-six years old, men came from Charan and told Rivkah about her brother, Lavan, son of Besuel, who had, until then, been childless. Neither did any of his maidservants have children. Then God remembered Adina, the wife of Lavan, and she gave birth to twin daughters. The older one was called Leah and the younger one, Rachel. Rivkah was extremely happy to learn about her brother's children.

YITZCHAK'S BLESSINGS

Yitzchak was now advanced in years and his eyesight weakened. He called his son, Eisav, and asked him to gather his hunting gear and go off to the field and hunt and bring him meat and savory dishes. He would then give him his blessing, as his life was apparently nearing its end. Eisav went to hunt for venison to bring to his father and thus receive the blessing.

Meanwhile, Rivkah had heard this and she hurried to her son, Yaakov, telling him what his father had planned. She said, "Now obey me and go to the sheep and take two young kids and I shall prepare savory dishes for your father before your brother returns." Yaakov did not wish to do this but his mother prevailed upon him to obey her. She hurried to get the meat ready before Eisav's return. She also clothed Yaakov with Eisav's garments and put the goat's skins on Yaakov's hands and on the smooth nape of his neck to simulate the hairy skin of Eisav.

Yaakov came to his father and his father asked him, "Who are you?" and he replied, "I am your firstborn, Eisav." He asked his father to sit and eat what he had brought him. Yitzchak ate and was very happy and he blessed Yaakov.

As soon as Yaakov had left, Eisav came in with his catch of venison and asked his father to eat and to bless him. Yitzchak, now very agitated, asked, "Who was it that had come and brought venison which I ate before you entered and I did bless him — let the blessing stand." Eisav was livid with rage and said, "Indeed he is rightly called Yaakov since he has now supplanted me twice. He took away my right as first-born and now he has taken my blessing." Eisav wept bitterly. Yitzchak said, "Your brother came with guile and took your blessing."

Eisav now hated Yaakov over these blessings and Yaakov was, therefore, told by his mother to depart until his brother's anger abated. So Yaakov fled to the home of Ever, son of Shem, and stayed there for fourteen years. Eisav also left and settled in Seir. There he saw a woman named Bosmas, daughter of Eilon the Hittite and took her as a wife in addition to his other wives. Eisav called her Adah, implying that the blessings had been removed from him. There he remained for six months, seeing neither his father nor mother. He then brought these wives back to Chevron where they constantly provoked Yitzchak and Rivkah by their deeds. They worshiped idols of stone and wood and burned incense to them.

Rivkah said to her husband, "I am weary to death on account of these Hittite women. Should Yaakov, too, marry such, my life would not be worth living." Then Adah, wife of Eisav, gave birth to a son, Eliphaz, when Eisav was sixty-five years old.

Yishmael, son of Avraham, died when Yaakov was sixty-five years old. Yishmael had lived for one hundred thirty- seven years and his brother, Yitzchak, mourned him for many days.

Yaakov, now in the academy of Ever, longed to see his parents. Until this time, Eisav had not thought much about the incident of the blessings. But when Yaakov came and Eisav saw him, his hatred was revived and he said, "The mourning time of my father will soon arrive, then I will kill my brother, Yaakov." Rivkah was told of the evil intention of her older son against the younger one. She told Yaakov to flee to Charan and to stay there for a time with her brother, Lavan, until Eisav's anger would have cooled.

Yitzchak sent for Yaakov and forbade him to marry any woman of Canaan. He told him that his own father, Avraham, had charged him to observe the ways of God and that He should not be forsaken. "Do not take a wife from this land, but arise and go to Charan, to the house of Besuel, your mother's father, and take a wife of Lavan's daughters."

He implored him not to copy the habits of the land in which he was now to reside, but to continue always in the fear of God and that God would show him mercy and would give him and his descendants the blessing of Avraham and he would become a congregation of peoples. He told him that one day God would bring him back to his native land in happiness. Then after blessing Yaakov, he gave him many gifts of gold and silver and sent him on his way. Yaakov obeyed his parents and left after kissing them. He went on his way to Paddan-Aram. He was seventy-seven on his departure from Be'er Sheva.

Eliphaz Overtakes Yaakov

Yaakov started on his journey. Eisav knew about this and summoned his own son, Eliphaz, who was at that time a boy of thirteen years. He commanded Eliphaz, "Go and follow Yaakov. When you reach him, kill him and take all his possessions." Eliphaz obeyed. He, too, was a good hunter and expert with a bow and arrow. Eliphaz took with him ten men who were brothers of his mother. He pursued his uncle, Yaakov, and overtook him on the border of Canaan near the city of Shechem.

Yaakov was taken aback at the sight of this company hunting him and he stopped, having no idea of what was to happen. Yaakov asked Eliphaz the meaning of this and Eliphaz then drew his sword and told Yaakov, "My father commanded me to kill you and I must fulfill his orders." Yaakov realized that this matter was a strong order from Eisav. Yaakov tried to persuade Eliphaz to take all that he had but not to kill him.

God intervened by making Eliphaz and his men have pity on Yaakov, whom they stripped of all his belongings. Then Eliphaz and his escort returned to Be'er Sheva. Yaakov's possessions were given to Eisav, who was very angry at his son for not having killed Yaakov. So Eisav took the riches and placed them in his house.

Eisav knew that Yitzchak had blessed Yaakov before the latter's departure and had charged him not to take a wife from the daughters of Canaan, since these were displeasing to his parents. So Eisav went to the house of Yishmael, his uncle, and took a wife, Machalas, daughter of Yishmael, the sister of Nevayos and he married her in addition to the wives which he already had.

Vayeitzei

Yaakov in Charan

Yaakov left his home and proceeded towards Charan. He made his way to Mount Moriah and spent the night at that place which was near the town of Luz. God appeared to him during the night and said to him, "I am the God of Avraham and Yitzchak, your father. The land on which you now lie, I will give to you and to your children. I am with you. Do not fear. I shall guard you wherever you go. I shall increase your offspring as the stars of heaven and I shall bring you back to this land with children and wealth."

Yaakov awoke from his sleep and was happy on account of this vision. He named that place "Beis-Eil." He was so content that he continued his journey with light steps. He went to the Land of the Sons of the East and when he came to Charan, he rested near a well which was frequented by the shepherds of the area. He saw men proceeding from the direction of Charan to feed their sheep. He asked them where they came from and they told him that they had come from Charan, whereupon he asked whether they knew Lavan, son of Nachor. They said that they knew him and that all was well with him and that his daughter, Rachel, was about to arrive with her father's sheep, as she was a shepherdess.

Yaakov Meets Rachel

While Yaakov was still talking with these shepherds, Rachel arrived. When Yaakov saw her, he ran towards her and kissed her and he raised his voice and cried. Yaakov told Rachel that he was the son of her father's sister and she immediately went to tell her father, Lavan, about this visitor. Yaakov continued weeping as he had brought no gifts to Lavan's house (as did Eliezer, servant of Avraham, who had taken his mother from this land). When Lavan heard that his nephew had come, he met him and embraced him and brought him into his house and gave him food and drink.

Then Yaakov told Lavan how Eliphaz, son of Eisav, had pursued him and robbed him. Yaakov had stayed with Lavan for one month as his guest, when Lavan said, "Let us now discuss the details of your hire, as you will work for me. I do not wish you to serve me without payment." Lavan had two daughters and, at that time, he had no sons. His wife, Adinah, had borne him these two daughters, Leah the elder, and Rachel, the younger. The eyes of Leah were weak but Rachel was beautiful in appearance and Yaakov loved her. So Yaakov said, "I will work for you for seven years for your daughter, Rachel, to be my wife." Lavan agreed.

Now in the second year of the stay of Yaakov in Charan which was in the seventy-ninth year of his life, Ever, son of Shelach, died at the age of four hundred and forty-six and Yaakov mourned for his teacher for many days. In the third year of his stay in Charan, Bosmas, the daughter of Yishmael and wife of Eisav, bore him a son who was named Reu'el. In the fourth year of his stay with Lavan, God remembered Lavan on Yaakov's account and sons were born to his wife. The oldest of these was Be'or. Then came Eliv and Morash. Lavan was now rich in children and worldly possessions.

YAAKOV AND LAVAN

In those days, Yaakov worked for Lavan and performed every form of labor, both in the house and in the field. Indeed, God's blessing was apparent in Lavan's home. In the fifth year of Yaakov's sojourn with his uncle, Yehudis, daughter of Be'eri, the wife of Eisav, died in Canaan. She had no sons but she had daughters. Their names were Marzis and Puis. Then Eisav took courage and went to the region of Seir in order to hunt. During the sixth year of Yaakov's stay in Charan, Eisav married Oholivamah, daughter of Anah, daughter of Tzivon the Chivite. Eisav brought her to Canaan and she gave birth to Ye'ush, Ya'alam and Korach.

There was, at that time, a battle in Canaan between the shepherds of Eisav's flocks and the shepherds of the land of

Canaan. Eisav had so much, that the territory was not wide enough for him and his possessions. He realized that the situation was not to be overcome, so he took his family and all his belongings and went to Seir. Yet, from time to time, Eisav would return to Canaan to visit his parents. Eisav also made connections with the Chorite clan by giving his daughters to the sons of the Chorites as wives. These were the sons of Seir the Chorite. He gave his daughter, Marzis, in marriage to Anah, the son of Tzivon, his wife's brother. Puis married Eitzer, son of Bilhon the Chorite and Eisav remained in Seir for some time and prospered there.

YAAKOV MARRIES LEAH

In the seventh year of Yaakov's stay with Lavan, his term of work ended and he asked Lavan for his daughter, Rachel, as stipulated. So Lavan assembled all the people of the place and made the wedding feast. During the feast, Lavan arrived with his friends who began to extinguish the lamps one by one. Yaakov wondered, "What is the meaning of this?" and was told, "This is an old custom in our country." Then Lavan took his older daughter, Leah, and brought her to Yaakov. Lavan gave Leah one of his servants, Zilpah, as a handmaid. Everyone knew of Lavan's trick, but they all kept the secret. Then they came to eat and make merry to the sound of drums and they all sang in chorus, "Heliah, Heliah." Yaakov assumed this was also the custom in that place. It was now completely dark.

When morning came, Yaakov realized that he had been deceived and he now understood the meaning of the strange chorus, "Heliah," which meant, "She is Leah." When he complained about this deception, Lavan explained that it was against the custom of the place to marry off the younger before the older, but if he wished to marry Rachel, he could do so for a further seven years' service. Yaakov accepted the offer and was given Rachel as a wife. Now he loved Rachel more than he loved Leah. Lavan also gave Rachel a maid servant named Bilhah.

When God saw that Leah was not favored by Yaakov, he let

her have children and she bore four sons; Reuven, Shimon, Levi and Yehudah. Then she stopped bearing children for some time. Rachel was childless and envied her sister. So Rachel took her servant, Bilhah, and gave her to Yaakov as a wife and she bore him two sons; Dan and Naphtali. Then Leah, too, gave her servant, Zilpah, to Yaakov as a wife and she bore two sons; Gad and Asher. But Leah did bear children again; two sons, Yisachar and Zevulun, and a daughter, Dinah. Rachel, in her distress, prayed to God, not to let her remain childless and to give her at least what the maid servants had — two sons!

Rachel was remembered by God and she gave birth to a son, who she named Yoseif from the word "asaph," meaning that God had withdrawn her shame and also from "yasaph," meaning that God would add another son to this one. Yaakov was ninety-one when Yoseif was born. At this time, his mother, Rivkah, sent him Devorah, daughter of Utz who had been her nurse, who had come from Charan with her when she married Yitzchak. With Devorah also came two of Yitzchak's servants. Their purpose was to tell Yaakov that the time had arrived for him to return to his parents, to the land of Canaan. Yaakov took note of this since his seven years of service for Rachel had ended at that very time.

Now, at the end of fourteen years with Lavan, Yaakov said to his father-in-law, "Give me my wives and let me go to my country, since my mother has sent word that I should return." Lavan answered, "If it pleases you, stay on. State the amount that you wish for your hire for the work you have done for me." So Yaakov stipulated that he would continue working, if he were allowed to visit Lavan's flock and take from these all the speckled and spotted sheep and goats and those which were dark-skinned. Lavan agreed. Yaakov handed all these spotted sheep to his sons to shepherd and he, himself, tended to the remaining sheep of Lavan. Yitzchak's servants, who had come to fetch Yaakov home, saw that he was not ready to return with them. They left him and returned to Canaan, but the nurse, Devorah, stayed on at Charan, with Yaakov's wives.

Yaakov worked a further six years in order to earn the sheep. He took aside the spotted ones as soon as they were born. He became rich, having servants, sheep, camels and donkeys. He had in all two hundred thousand droves of sheep. These sheep were very big and fertile and men offered huge sums for just one of these. They would exchange a servant, a camel or donkey for just one of Yaakov's sheep. Lavan's sons became jealous of Yaakov saying that he had become wealthy by taking their father's sheep. Yaakov noticed that Lavan was no longer well-disposed towards him.

YAAKOV DEPARTS

At this time, when the six years were over and Yaakov had been with Lavan for twenty years, God appeared to Yaakov and told him to leave Charan and return to his native land. So Yaakov took his wives and children and all his sheep to return to Canaan.

Lavan had, at this time, gone to shear his sheep of the wool. Meanwhile, Yaakov left to return to Canaan. Rachel took her fathers *teraphim*-idols and hid them on the camel where she sat. These *teraphim* were an abomination. The heathens made these from gold and silver in the form of a man and at certain times of the day (known to the makers of these) they would absorb celestial influences and would foretell the future. Rachel took those belonging to Lavan, her father, for a certain reason. She wished to deprive him of the power of discovering the direction which Yaakov had taken when he left.

When Lavan returned to his home he discovered that Yaakov and his family were not there. He went to the *teraphim* to discover his whereabouts, but these had also disappeared. He had recourse to other people's *teraphim* and he was told that Yaakov had left for the land of Canaan. Lavan took his kinsmen with him and overtook Yaakov and his camp at Gilead. Lavan began to remonstrate with Yaakov and said, "What have you done to me by fleeing and leading my daughters away as if they were war captives? You gave me no opportunity to kiss my own daughters farewell and you stole my gods." Yaakov told him that he feared that he would take his daughters from him if he told him that he was leaving, but should anyone be found to have stolen the idols, that person would be killed. After searching the tents, Lavan did not find the idols, since, as had been mentioned, Rachel had hidden them in the trappings of the camel on which she was sitting.

Then Lavan said, "Let us make a covenant between us that you shall not ill-treat my daughters, nor will you take any other wives besides them, and that God be a witness between us." They took stones and made these into a heap and Lavan said, "This heap will be a witness between us." So they called the place Galed (*gal*-heap, and *ed*-witness). They both offered sacrifices on the mount and they spent the night at that place. Lavan arose in the morning and blessed his daughters and their children and kissed them and each went his way.

Now Lavan returned to Charan, but retaining his cunning and his spite, he sent his seventeen year old son, Be'or, with Avichor, son of Utz, son of Nachor and ten other men on the following mission. They were to avoid Yaakov's track, but to go by another route to Seir, Eisav's dwelling place. Upon reaching this place they were to speak to Eisav as follows, "So says your kinsman, your mother's brother, Lavan. Do you know what your brother, Yaakov, did to me? He came to me almost naked and I brought him to my own home. I made him rich. When I had left to shear my sheep, he took everything with him to return to his father in Canaan. He also stole my gods. I left him at the brook Yabok and I took nothing from him. Should you wish to apprehend him there, do so now. Do to him as you see fit."

Eisav Prepares for Battle

Eisav's old anger against Yaakov was now rekindled. He took with him sixty men and in addition, he collected from the clan of Seir, the Chorite, three hundred and forty men, making four hundred in all. They were armed with sharp swords for the fight against Yaakov. Eisav divided his camps into seven companies and took members of his own retinue — sixty — and placed them under the command of his son, Eliphaz. The six other companies were placed under the Chorite command.

After their meeting with Eisav in Seir, Lavan's messengers continued to Rivkah, and told her about this imminent conflict and of Eisav's intention to slay Yaakov. Rivkah then took seventy-two of Yitzchak's servants and told them to meet with Yaakov at Yabok. Yaakov looked upon this company as a camp sent from God to help him. He, therefore, called the place "Machanayim" (two camps). He recognized his father's men and he welcomed them and wept with them as he spoke with them about his parent's welfare.

They then related to Yaakov the following message from his mother. "Your mother sends these men to you. I have heard, my son, that your brother, Eisav, is about to meet you with the men of Seir. Now, obey me, and when you meet him, deal with him in a conciliatory manner. Do not utter hostile words to him. Give a gift of what you have — that with which God has favored you. Hide nothing from him if he asks about your affairs. He may change his hostile intentions and you will preserve your own life. He is your older brother and, for this alone, you owe him respect."

When Yaakov heard these words from his mother's messengers, he wept bitterly. He resolved to do exactly as his mother had commanded him.

Vayishlach

Yaakov's Messengers

Now Yaakov sent messengers to his brother, Eisav, to the land of Seir. This he did in order to discuss matters in a peaceful manner. Yaakov ordered these messengers as follows, "So shall you speak to Eisav. 'Thus says your servant, Yaakov. Do not think that the blessings of our father have benefited me. I have been at Lavan's house for twenty years. He has deceived me again and again by changing the terms of my hire. I toiled for him and he used me to the full extent until God saw my troubles and travail and caused him to change his attitude towards me. Now I have oxen and sheep and herds only because of God's mercy. As I approach my native land and my parents, I am sending you these messengers to inform you so that I may be received graciously by you. Again I insist that you do not believe that I have gained all this wealth on account of the blessing of our father.'"

These messengers met Eisav and his army of four hundred Chorite swordsmen on the border of Edom while he was on his way to confront Yaakov. They delivered their message to Eisav to which Eisav replied in an arrogant and abusive manner. "I have indeed heard how Yaakov has treated Lavan. Lavan made him rich, and gave him his two daughters who bore him children. How he fled with those children and carried away Lavan's daughters, as if they were captives. Yaakov did this not only to Lavan but to me, too. He deceived me twice and I remained silent. Now, I come with my company and shall do to him as I have planned."

The messengers returned to Yaakov and told him as follows: "We came to your brother and told him what you ordered us to tell him, but he comes towards you with four hundred men. We advise you to pray to God to save you."

Yaakov heard this and was greatly distressed. He prayed, "God of Avraham and of Yitzchak, my father, Who told me when I left my father's house that He would give me this land to inherit and make my offspring numerous and that I would spread forth to the four corners of the earth. You have fulfilled Your promise by giving me wealth and children. You also said, 'return to your native land and I shall confer good upon you. You delivered me from Lavan, but I now fall into the hands of Eisav, who wishes to kill me and my children. Deliver me from him. I have no merit of my own, but do this for the sake of Avraham and Yitzchak."

Yaakov ended this prayer and he divided his company into two camps. One was placed with Damesek, son of Eliezer, Avraham's servant, and with some of his own sons and the second with Elinos, Eliezer's other son. He told them, "Keep a distance from each other so that if Eisav comes to one camp to attack it, the other might escape."

A Heavenly Army

Yaakov spent the night in that place, giving instructions about his children and his possessions. God heard his prayer and He sent three angels to confront Eisav. As the angels appeared to him, he looked up and there, in front of him, he saw what appeared to him as thousands of men on horseback, all heavily armed, and forming four divisions. Thus did they appear to all the men of Eisav's army. One of these divisions confronted Eisav and while his company of four hundred men were totally confused, Eisav, himself, fell from his horse. Then these heavenly armies left him where he was, but they told him as follows: "We are the servants of Yaakov, servant of God. No one will be able to stand before such a mighty army?" Eisav cried out, "Brother Yaakov, I have not seen you for twenty years. I have come to greet you and this is what you do to me?" The angels said to him, "It is only because your brother is Yaakov that you are alive, and if not for this fact, not one of your company would be saved."

The first division left Eisav. Eisav and his army had gone one *parsah's* distance when a second company arrived and frightened

Eisav as the first one had. Eisav cried out again, "Master Yaakov. I have come to greet you and this is what you do to me?" The troop replied as the first one had replied. Then a third army came and a fourth, and each did as the first had done.

Eisav now decided to approach his brother peaceably. He concealed his hatred for his brother because he was now very much afraid for his life. Yaakov spent the night taking counsel with his servants about how to deal with his brother. He took four hundred and forty sheep, camels, donkeys, goats, oxen and cows, arranging them in ten herds, each led by one of his servants. They were told to leave a space between each herd. He told them, "If Eisav asked to whom these belong, tell him that you, yourselves, are servants of Yaakov and that you are on a mission to meet Eisav and that Yaakov is behind you. This is a present sent to you from your brother." If Eisav should ask why is Yaakov so far behind, you must say, "It is because he wishes to meet you joyfully, therefore he first sends this gift to appease you before greeting you personally."

YAAKOV'S WRESTLES

Yaakov's gift passed on before him led by the servants, and he spent that night at a ford, Yabok. Yaakov arose at midnight and took his wives and children and all his belongings and made them cross the shallow river. He was now left on his own. Suddenly, a man came and wrestled with him until dawn. During this struggle the hollow of Yaakov's thigh was dislocated. Then the man, who could not prevail over him, left him and blessed him. Yaakov crossed over the ford at dawn as he limped because of his dislocated thigh. Then the sun shone as he pressed on from Yabok. At midday, they all journeyed, and Yaakov lifted his eyes and saw Eisav was approaching with his men. He divided his sons and wives and servants and he placed his daughter, Dinah, in a box, giving her into the safekeeping of his servants. He went on alone to meet Eisav, bowing seven times, as he approached him.

THE BROTHERS MEET

God caused Eisav to be gracious and compassionate towards Yaakov. Eisav feared Yaakov on account of his experience with the armies of angels. Eisav ran towards his brother and embraced and kissed him and they both wept. Likewise, all Eisav's men embraced Yaakov, together with Eliphaz, Eisav's oldest son, who was with his four brothers. Eisav then saw Yaakov's wives and children and asked, "Who are these?" Yaakov said, "These are my children, given to me graciously by God. They are here to find grace in your eyes." Then Yaakov asked Eisav to accept the gift of cattle. Eisav said, "Why so, my brother, I have enough. Keep what is yours." But Yaakov prevailed on his brother to accept the gift, because, "I have seen you and you received me graciously." Yaakov also gave gifts of silver and gold and urged Eisav to accept them, which he did.

Eisav divided the cattle among the men with him; half to his own sons and half to his servants. He gave the precious jewels and silver and gold to his son, Eliphaz. Eisav said to Yaakov "Let us stay together and we shall journey slowly until you arrive at my place and we shall then dwell together." Yaakov said, "So I would do, but you must know that the children are tender and the flocks and herds must travel slowly. You are aware that this is my task. If they are driven on, they will perish. So proceed before me and I shall make my way slowly until I reach my master at Seir." Eisav said, "I shall place some of my men with you to ease your burden." Yaakov declined this offer, but said that eventually he would join him. Yaakov wished to place a distance between Eisav and his own men, so as to get to his father in Canaan as soon as possible.

Eisav then returned with his four hundred men to Seir. Yaakov and his family went to the border of Canaan and stayed there a few days. Then he crossed into the land of Shalem to the city of Shechem and encamped before that city. He bought a parcel of land from Chamor's sons and paid five shekels. He called the place 'Sukkos' meaning 'booths' since he had built booths there for his cattle. He lived in this place for one year and six months.

The Abduction of Dinah

At that time, the women of the city of Shechem went out to dance and make merry. Rachel and Leah also went with their servant-women and sat there watching. Among the important people present at this gathering was the prince Shechem, son of Chamor, the ruler of that land. Shechem saw Dinah, the daughter of Yaakov and Leah, while she was sitting with her mother. She pleased Shechem greatly and he asked his friends, "Who is that girl. She seems to be a stranger; I have never seen her before." They told him, "She is Dinah, the daughter of Yaakov, a descendant of Avraham, the Hebrew. She now lives here with her family." Upon hearing this Shechem abducted her, and defiled and humiliated her. He forced her stay with him in his palace.

This matter was made known to Yaakov who sent two of his servants to bring back Dinah, but these were driven away. Shechem and his men embraced her in the presence of Yaakov's men. The servants returned to Yaakov and reported to him the manner of their reception and the treatment of Dinah. Yaakov contained his anger until his sons' return from the field. Meanwhile he sent two girls of the servants' daughters to keep Dinah company. Then Shechem sent three of his friends to Chamor, his father, asking him to obtain Dinah as his wife. Chamor, son of Chidkam the Chivite, came to his son's house and sat with him. He asked his son, "Are there no young women among our own people so that you must take a Hebrew girl?" Shechem replied, "I wish to marry only her." Chamor yielded to his son's request, as he loved him very much.

Yaakov's sons had hastily arrived from the field not even waiting to gather in all the sheep. They had heard what had happened to their sister and were aghast. At once they told their father that Shechem had incurred the death penalty, since God had commanded the sons of Noach against robbery and adultery. Not one person in the whole city of Shechem had protested. "The whole city has to die, since not one of them raised his voice in opposition."

As they were talking, Chamor, the father of Shechem arrived in order to discuss his son's request with Yaakov. He sat before Yaakov and his family. Chamor explained that his son desired to marry Dinah. "You will intermarry with us, giving us your daughters, and we shall also give you ours; you may dwell with us and become one people with us in our land; the country is spacious and you may trade in it and no one will complain."

Chamor ended his talk and his son, Shechem, joined him. "May I find favor with you," he said "I shall do whatever you ask. You may ask for a high dowry — as much as you desire — but give me this young woman as a wife." Yaakov's sons answered with guile. "Meanwhile, our sister is still in your house," they pointed out, "and we must also send word to our grandfather, Yitzchak, to consult with him in this matter; we are unable to act in such a matter without his advice." They did this as a stalling tactic in order to seek a way of dealing with Shechem and his people. They sought a suitable means of punishing the whole city.

Shimon said, "Here is some advice. Tell them that every male must be circumcised, just as we are. If they do not consent to this, we shall take our sister and depart. Let them do what we ask and when they are weak from the operation, we shall attack them."

Eventually, Chamor and Shechem returned to the house of Yaakov and were told what Yitzchak had advised. "No one of Avraham's descendants were to marry into uncircumcised families," they said. They would consent to the marriage and dwell with them if they all agreed to be circumcised.

Chamor heard this and was pleased. He came before the assembled inhabitants of his land and spoke as follows: "These men are willing to dwell with us and to intermarry with us only if we agree to be circumcised. They will then be one with us. Their cattle and possessions are ours." The people consented to this since both Chamor and Shechem were esteemed there. During the following day and the day after, all the men of Shechem were circumcised. Chamor and Shechem, with his five brothers were all circumcised. The number of men who underwent this procedure were six hundred forty-four, and the children numbered two hundred seventy-six.

Chidkam, the son of Pered, father of Chamor and his six brothers did not take the advice of the others and refused to be circumcised. They were annoyed that this was done by the men of the city. On the second day towards the evening, eight children were found who had been hidden by their mothers. Chamor and his son sent for these to have them circumcised. But Chidkam and his six brothers sprang on the men with words and prevented this. They said to Shechem, "Must you marry a Hebrew girl? Are there not enough Canaanite women that you must do this thing which is unknown to us? What will you say when the dwellers of this land discover what you have done? This is unknown to us and to our ancestors. We shall smite you for this and leave you with nothing." Then Chamor and Shechem replied. "We did not do this out of love for the Hebrews. We had no alternative. Once we have recovered, we will know how do deal with these Hebrews."

These words were overheard by Dinah, who commanded one of the girls who had been sent to her by her father. She was to inform her father and brothers of the evil intention of the men of that city. Yaakov received this message and became enraged. On hearing the news, Shimon and Levi took an oath that nothing would be left of that city.

Shimon and Levi's Revenge

As the battle began, twenty young men of Shechem who had hidden and had not been circumcised fought with Shimon and Levi. They were dealt with quickly and only two escaped, hiding in the nearby lime pits. Then Shimon and Levi fell upon the inhabitants of the city of Shechem until none were left. Chamor and his son, Shechem, were killed and Dinah was taken from their home. The brothers were then attacked by three hundred stone-throwing women whom Shimon and Levi quickly killed.

They then returned to their father. When he saw them and the spoil, he became very angry and said, "What have you done to me. I have, at last, found rest and now you put me to shame among the dwellers of Canaan. They, with the Perizzites, will gather against me and destroy my house. We are already few in number." The brothers replied, "Shall one be allowed to deal with our sister as with a harlot?" Eighty-five women were taken captive. One girl, named Bunah, was taken by Shimon and became his wife. Forty-seven males were taken and not killed and they remained with Yaakov until he and his family left for Egypt.

After the two brothers had attacked and sacked the city, the two uncircumcised boys who were hidden in the lime pits came out. When they made their way back to the city of Shechem, they found utter desolation. They could only guess as to what had happened.

They made their way to a nearby city called Tappuach and reported the matter to its king, Yashuv. He wished to verify the statement of the two boys, since he could not, of course, believe what they had told them. The king received reports from his men that the city was truly in ruins. King Yashuv remarked, "Such a thing has never been heard of since the days of Nimrod. How can two men obliterate an entire city? Let us, at once, take revenge of these Hebrews for what they have done to the city of Shechem." His advisors, however, told him, "You will never vanquish these Hebrews. These brothers possess extraordinary powers. All the surrounding kings should be notified and with our combined strength, we will make an invincible army." So Yashuv called together the kings of the Amorites, who were astonished, as well.

THE AMORITES PREPARE FOR BATTLE

Seven Amorite kings assembled with about ten thousand swordsmen. They came to do battle with the sons of Yaakov. When Yaakov heard this, he again rebuked his two sons. "You have brought all the dwellers of the land against me." Yehudah replied, "Do you think that Shimon and Levi did this for no reason? A great crime was committed and for this reason, God caused them to be victorious. The same God will also give us victory over these attackers." He asked his father to pray to God on behalf of their cause.

Then Yehudah sent spies to discover where these kings were encamped with their armies. The servants scouted and observed that the Amorite armies were in the vicinity of Mount Zion. Yehudah, on discovering this, told his brothers to take courage. They were to gird themselves with their armor and be prepared. They were joined by their servants and the servants of Yitzchak from Chevron and they numbered in all one hundred and twelve men. Yaakov also went with them.

Then they sent messages to Yitzchak at ChevronKiryas Arba saying, "Pray for us to our God to save us from the enemy who wishes to destroy us." Yitzchak prayed as follows, "God, Who promised my father, Avraham, to multiply us, hear me. The kings of the Amorites assemble to do battle with my children. Frustrate the counsel of these kings and put the fear of my children into them. Bring down their pride and make them retreat."

Yaakov also prayed, "O God Who reigns over all from the beginning of time and for all time. You may cause war, but are also able to suppress war. Put fear into the hearts of these kings and make them desist from their plan. Bring low their pride and place dread into the hearts of their camps."

The Amorite kings came and waited in the field in full battle array. A sudden fear of the sons of Yaakov descended upon them. Their advisors told them, "It would be foolish to wage war because the God of these men will not forsake them. Remember how Avraham was saved from Nimrod and how that same Avraham fought the five kings of Eilam in order to save his nephew, Lot. This very victory was accomplished by a few men. Then," they continued, "there was the sacrifice of Yitzchak where God intervened and promised Avraham to save his sons from any evil which may threaten them." They mentioned the incidents of Pharaoh of Egypt and Avimelech of Gerar when they wished to take Sarah as a wife, and how Eisav with his four hundred men came with intent to kill, but Yaakov was saved by his God.

"This same God," they concluded, "will now save Yaakov and his sons. It is God who gave strength to these sons to defeat Shechem, since no two humans have ever achieved such a victory. Even a thousand times the number of troops you have assembled here could not defeat them." These words carried weight with the kings and they took the advice offered them and did not fight with the sons of Yaakov. They all returned to their places. The sons of Yaakov waited until the evening at Mount Zion and when no attack began, they saw that it was safe for them to return home.

At that time, God appeared to Yaakov and said, "Arise and go to Beis-Eil and dwell there. Make an altar to the God Who appeared to you and Who delivered you and your sons." Yaakov took his sons and all his possessions and came to Beis-Eil. He was now ninety-nine years old. He went to Beis-Eil, which was Luz, and built an altar there and remained there for six months. At that time, Devorah, daughter of Utz, the nurse of Rivkah, died and was buried beneath the oak below Beis-Eil. This place was called Allon Bachus — the oak of weeping.

Now Rivkah, daughter of Besuel, mother of Yaakov, died in Chevron-Kiryas Arba and was buried in the cave of Machpelah. which Avraham had brought from the Hittites. Rivkah had lived one hundred and thirty-three years. Yaakov heard about this and mourned greatly. Devorah, the nurse of Rivkah, was still alive when Rivkah died and she joined in the mourning and when that nurse died, too, this place was indeed "Allon Bachus," "oak of mourning."

Lavan of Aram, Yaakov's father-in-law, died at that time. He was punished by God because he had broken the covenant made with Yaakov (by having sent men with a treacherous message to Eisav as has been narrated).

The Death of Rachel

When Yaakov was one hundred years old, God appeared to him and named him Yisrael (champion of God). Rachel, his wife, was about to give birth to a child on the way to Ephras where she died in childbirth. Yaakov buried her in that place and placed a monument over her grave which is there to this day. She died at the age of forty-five. Yaakov called this son, whom she had borne, Binyamin, "son of the right," since he had been born in the direction called *yamin* which is south.

When Rachel died, Yaakov moved his dwelling to the tent of Bilhah, Rachel's maid-servant, and Reuven, Leah's son, became very annoyed. He went into that tent and cut down his father's bed. This act cost him his birthright, the monarchy and the priesthood. The birthright was now given to Yoseif, the monarchy to Yehudah and the priesthood to Levi.

Yaakov's Children

These are the generations of Yaakov who were born in Padan Aram. He had twelve sons. The sons of Leah were Reuven, Shimon, Levi, Yehudah, Yisachar, Zevulun and Dinah, their sister. The sons of Rachel were Yoseif and Binyamin. The sons of Zilpah were Gad and Asher and those of Bilhah were Dan and Naphtali.

Now Yaakov journeyed with all his family and came to Mamrei, which is Kiryas Arba in Chevron, where Avraham and Yitzchak had dwelt. Yaakov and his family settled in Chevron and lived with his father Yitzchak. Eisav, his brother, together with his family and all his possessions, journeyed to Seir. There they settled and multiplied.

Eisav's Descendants

These are the generations of Eisav borne to him in Canaan. Eisav had five sons. His wife, Adah, bore to him Eliphaz. His wife, Bosmas, bore to him Reu'el. And his wife, Oholivamah, bore to him Ye'ush, Ya'alam and Korach. The sons of Eliphaz were Teman, Omar, Tsefo, Gaatom, Kenaz and Amalek. The sons of Reu'el were Nachas, Zerach, Shamma and Mizah. The sons of Ye'ush were Timna, Alva and Yeseis. The sons of Ya'alam were Eilah, Pinon and Kenaz. The sons of Korach were Teman, Omar, Mivtzar, Magdiel and Iram. These are the descendants of Eisav at Seir.

Seir's Descendants

These are the names of children of Seir the Chorite, dwellers of the land of Seir: Lotan, Shoval, Tzivon, Anah, Dishon, Eitzer and Dishan — seven in all. The sons of Lotan were Chori, Heiman and a sister, Timna. This Timna had once come to Yaakov and his sons, but they paid no attention to her. She then went to Eliphaz, son of Eisav, and bore him a son, Amalek. The sons of Shoval were Alvan, Monachas, Eival, Seto and Onam. The sons of Tzivon were Ayah and Anah. Anah, had discovered the *Yeimim* in the wilderness while he was tending the donkeys of his father, Tzivon.

Anah Finds the Yeimim

Anah had taken his father's donkeys to a deserted place near the banks of the Red Sea. Suddenly, a strong wind blew in from the sea which caused the animals to stop — frozen with fear. A moment later, about one hundred and twenty strange, terrifying beasts came charging out of the wilderness. From the middle part of their bodies downwards they took the form of humans. From that part upwards some looked like bears, others like apes. They had tails behind their shoulders like the tails of hoopoes. These monstrous beasts came and rode on the donkeys and disappeared entirely into the wilderness.

One of these beasts, or 'Yeimim,' came near to Anah and struck him with its tail and Anah fled in fright. When he reached Seir, he told his father, Tzivon, about this amazing spectacle. No one was ever able to find these creatures, and Anah and his brothers never again went to that place — they feared for their lives.

The children of Anah, son of Seir, were Dishon and his sister Oholivamah. The sons of Dishon were Utz and Aran. These were the families of the children of Seir, the Chorite.

Eisav and his sons lived in Seir and they took possession of that land and became numerous. Yaakov and his sons lived in Canaan as God had commanded their father, Avraham.

It was in the hundred and fifth year of the life of Yaakov, which is in the ninth year of his stay in Canaan, after returning from Padan Aram, that he and his sons returned to Shechem. They found good pasture land in that region and the city had been rebuilt after the onslaught by his sons. Three hundred men and women lived there, and Yaakov came to occupy the place which he had previously bought from Chamor.

THE BATTLE AT TAPPUACH

The kings of the Amorites and Canaanites heard that Yaakov and his sons had returned. They now assembled to fight against Yaakov. Yashuv, king of Tappuach, sent messengers to the neighboring kings: Eilon of Ga'ash, Iyhura of Shiloh, Peraason of Chasar, Susi of Sartan, Lavan of Beis-Choron and Sachir of Machanayim. "Come to me," he said, "and fight these Hebrews, for they wish to take my city." On hearing this, the kings marched with their armies and encamped near Tappuach. They arranged seven companies to fight against the family of Yaakov.

When word of this treachery reached Yaakov's sons, they girded their armor and took with them one hundred and twelve servants. Yaakov, himself, accompanied them. They took up their position in Tel-Shechem. Yaakov then bowed to God. "Almighty God," he prayed, "by Your mercy save your children from the enemy. Give my sons strength and courage and cause their enemies to fall before them."

Just as Yaakov ended his prayer, the earth trembled, the sun was obscured, and the kings became utterly confused. God caused a great commotion, similar to the sound of horses and chariots which sounded as if it had come from the camp of the Hebrews. They kings wanted to flee, but they remained, out of shame. They had fled from battle once before and did not wish to retreat again.

When the sons of Yaakov saw before them a huge army arrayed for war, they took up their weapons. Yehudah set out with ten men. He faced Yashuv, king of Tappuach, who was covered from head to foot by armor. Yashuv was a highly skilled warrior who was able to shoot arrows with both hands while riding a horse. This he could do in both directions, forward and backward at the same time. He never missed his target. This time, however, his hands were misguided by God. All the arrows which he shot struck his own men. He was still aiming at Yehudah who was only thirty cubits away from him, as Yehudah ran towards the king at full speed. Yehudah lifted a heavy stone from the ground, and, with all his might, hurled it at the king's shield. The king was thrown from his horse and his shield flew into the next division of soldiers. Then Yehudah advanced alone and slew forty-two men of Yashuv's company. Yashuv's entire army fled as he lay still on the ground in a daze. Suddenly he rose and engaged Yehudah in fierce hand-to-hand combat. Amidst clanging swords, blazing with fury, he struck at Yehudah's head with a spear. Yehudah's head was covered by a helmet which was split in two. Yehudah took his sword and aimed at Yashuv's legs, felling him, after which he cut off his head. Then Yaakov's other sons, encouraged by their brother's victory, killed 15,000 men. Yehudah then stripped the king of his armor. The enemy soldiers lost their courage to continue their fight and fled.

More Clashes

Then Levi spotted Eilon, king of Ga'ash, together with fourteen princes approaching for an attack. He slew these princes and Eilon singlehanded. As Iyhura, the king of Shiloh, came to assist his confederate, Yaakov shot an arrow and killed him. Four kings now remained. They were attacked by Yaakov's sons and fled in panic and disarray. Yet three of Yehudah's servants had been killed in battle and this angered Yehudah.

The enemy escaped and sought refuge in the city of Chasar. Yaakov's sons were held back in their attempt to enter the city by four soldiers. Naphtali quickly ran and killed two while the other two were killed by Yehudah. He now leaped onto the wall of Chasar followed by Shimon and Levi. The three quickly conquered the entire city and slew all the soldiers who had found refuge there. The inhabitants of Chasar implored the brothers to spare their lives. "Take anything you can find," they pleaded, "just do not kill us." The sons of Yaakov took the spoils and departed that same day. Then Yaakov, with his bow, killed Peraason of Chasar at the gate of his city. He then killed Susi of Sartan, Lavan, the king of Beis-Choron and Sachir of Machanayim while his sons continued the struggle against the remaining armies.

On the second day of the battle, the sons of Yaakov went to Sartan, since its dwellers were keen on avenging the death of their king, Susi. This city had huge walls with a moat surrounding it which was fifty cubits deep and forty cubits wide. This made it virtually impregnable! There was, however, a secret trail used only by the dwellers to enter the city which sons of Yaakov could not discover. There was also a drawbridge over the moat which was raised when it became known that the sons of Yaakov wished to enter the city. The citizens of Sartan were very much afraid, for they had heard what the sons of Yaakov had done to Chasar.

The sons of Yaakov were able to jump over the moat but could not enter the city, as the gates were of iron. It was impossible to break the wall down since the soldiers on the parapets hurled stones down at the attackers. The people shouted insults at the brothers which made them furious.

The brothers now planned a strategy. Yehudah went to the east of the city and Gad and Asher to the west side. While Shimon and Levi proceeded to the northern perimeter and Dan and Reuven took up positions on the south. Yisachar and Naphtali broke through the gates by setting fire to them and melting them. After a brief battle, the city of Sartan was taken and all resistance crumbled.

A number of warriors went into hiding in one of the high towers. Yehudah set fire to the tower and they all perished. Other men had found refuge in a distant fortress. Shimon and Levi went on the attack. Most of these soldiers surrendered immediately but twelve men resisted and fought back. One of these, with a lightning blow, struck Levi with his sword. Levi blunted the blow with his bare hand and grabbed the sword. He swiftly decapitated him — with his own sword. Now there were eleven warriors left. When they saw that their comrade had been killed, they were seized with rage. They pounced on Shimon and Levi like lions. The brothers realized that they could not win. What were they to do?

Shimon bellowed a fearful shout. The eleven men stood there — wide-eyed and confused. What was the meaning of this scream?

In the distance, Yehudah recognized his brother's voice, and he and Naphtali came to running to Shimon's aid. When they reached the scene, they found Shimon and Levi fighting a losing battle — they had no shields.

Naftali quickly handed each of them a shield. Yehudah joined in the fight. There were now three against eleven. They fought until nightfall, but they could not overcome their enemies.

When Yaakov learned of this battle, he was very troubled. He directed his prayers to God, and then, confidently, he and Naphtali went to help his three sons.

As he approached the battlefield, Yaakov drew his bow and instantly felled three of the warriors. The remaining eight, seeing that the tide was turning against them, fled as fast as their legs would carry them — to no avail — for the brothers pursued and killed all of them.

Now all of Yaakov's sons together searched the entire city of Sartan and they found twenty young men who had been hiding in a cave. Gad and Asher slew them. The remaining warriors, who had sought refuge in the fortress were slain by Dan and Naphtali. Of the entire population of Sartan, only the women and the children were spared.

The sons of Yaakov then went to Tappuach. Their king, Yashuv, had been slain but the people of this city were bent on fighting the sons of Yaakov. They were swiftly defeated. Then the city of Arbelyu had to be taken. In this case, even the women of the city were fighters. They heard the terrifying voices of the Hebrew brothers and fled. The women tried shooting stones in catapults from the walls but by the evening the city was taken by the sons of Yaakov. From there they went to Machanayim and defeated that city, too.

Victory at Ga'ash

On the fifth day, the sons of Yaakov heard that the people of Ga'ash were preparing to do battle against them. Undaunted, they donned their swords and armor and proceeded towards Ga'ash which was heavily fortified. It was the mightiest city of the Amorites, and was surrounded by three impregnable walls.

The sons of Yaakov found all the gates closed and on the outer wall there were 500 warriors on guard. Behind the walls, inside the city, there were countless other soldiers all ready for war.

As the sons of Yaakov tried to open the gates, the men who were arrayed behind the wall came forward and attacked. A bloody battle ensued. From the walls a rain of arrows and stones came down on the besieged sons.

Yehudah, seeing that the Ga'ashites were gaining the upper hand, let out a loud scream. The earsplitting sound astounded the defenders of the city to the extent that some fell from the wall. They were all dumbfounded, unable to move.

Yaakov's sons now launched their attack and slaughtered many of the enemy. But the citizens of Ga'ash who were inside the walls, regained their courage. They took the places of their fallen comrades on the walls and shot arrows and projectiles down at Yaakov's sons.

One of their men called out in a mocking tone: "Do you think that you will conquer Ga'ash as you did the other cities? Never! This battle will be your grave. We will take revenge for what you have done to the other cities!" Yehudah and his brothers heard these brazen words, and it made their blood boil. Yehudah called out, "Oh God, help us, Oh God, help us!"

Then he raced towards the wall and with one mighty jump, he vaulted to the top of the wall. There he stood — alone — surrounded by the enemy. As he sailed through the air, Yehudah somehow lost his sword — but he knew what to do.

He roared like a lion. Those on the wall were overcome with fright and ran for their lives. But there were some warriors who noted that Yehudah was unarmed. This they thought was their opportunity. They quickly surrounded him, and everyone drew his sword.

Yehudah, seeing death staring him in the face, called down to his brothers for help. Yaakov and his sons quickly drew their bows and, with perfect aim, slew three of the attackers. Again Yehudah roared. The remaining Amorites were so startled that they threw down their swords. Yehudah took one of the swords and boldly assaulted them, killing twenty of them within a matter of a few seconds.

Out of nowhere, a powerful fighter named Sarod appeared. He took careful aim for Yehudah's head and with his sword, split his helmet into two. Yehudah, although dazed, survived. Sarod, on seeing that he had failed, ran and fell from the wall onto the spears held by Yehudah's brothers.

Coming out of his stupor, Yehudah now sensed the pain in his head. He cried out in agony. Dan heard the cry, and filled with wrath, climbed up the wall, and stood beside his brother.

Now all the warriors fled to take refuge on the second, inner wall. From there they continued to shoot their arrows at the two brothers. Yaakov and his sons were unable to aim their arrows at these fighters, for the inner wall was out of their field of vision.

Yehudah and Dan, seeing no other way out, leaped onto the inner wall to do battle with the fighters there, and when the Amorites saw the heroic brothers, they took to their heels.

Meanwhile, hearing the shouts of the fleeing Amorites, and not being able to see what was happening, Yaakov and his sons became worried about the fate of Yehudah and Dan on the inner wall. This time Naphtali scaled the wall, while Yisachar and Zevulun breached the gates of the city, so that they could all enter.

Now, the final battle was joined. Yehudah, Dan and Naphtali who were on the wall, with their swords blazing, made their way down to their brothers on the ground and a veritable bloodbath ensued. Before long, an eerie silence fell over the entire city. Not one of the Amorites had survived the onslaught of Yaakov and his valiant sons.

Yaakov's sons now surveyed the devastated city of Ga'ash. Their thoughts dwelled on their lopsided victory. "They brought their ruin on themselves," they thought. "This is the fruit of unwarranted hatred."

Three Mighty Warriors

As they were musing the course of the war, out of nowhere three huge warriors appeared. Strangely, they carried no weapons. As Yaakov's sons approached them, one of the warriors sprang forward, grabbed Zevulun and, with all his might, hurled him to the ground.

At this incredible sight, Yaakov decided on swift retribution. With one stroke, the blade of his sword cut this warrior in two — his body fell on Zevulun.

The second warrior now leaped up to wrestle with Yaakov. Shimon and Levi swiftly cut him down. The third warrior, seeing the fate of his comrades, ran to the inner city, pursued by Yaakov's sons. As he ran for his life, he came upon a sword, still held by a fallen soldier. With this sword in his hand, he turned around to face Yaakov's sons. He struck at Yehudah's head but his sword glanced off the shield and Yehudah was unhurt. Shimon and Levi, the faithful brothers, finished him off. The three mighty warriors perished, together with all the other people of Ga'ash.

The Clash at Beis Chorin

There was to be no respite for the sons of Yaakov. As they climbed the hill to Beis Chorin, they were met by the inhabitants of that city. Dressed in battle gear, with their swords drawn, they were ready to fight. The battle lasted through the night. Yaakov's sons were vastly outnumbered, and they were not accustomed to night fighting.

Now they turned to God, crying out: "Help us, save us, Oh God. Let us not fall into their hands." God heard their prayer and He caused a great confusion to fall on the men of Beis Chorin. They fought furiously but they were fighting with each other. The noise of battle resounded, the earth trembled, the carnage was great, indeed.

Yaakov's sons watched from afar, and they understood that it was God's Hand that had brought about this miracle. When the morning dawned, the men of Beis Chorin had killed each other.

The Canaanites, the Chittites, the Amorites and Chivites heard this thundering noise throughout that night and they said, "This must be the Hebrews fighting against the cities. Who can withstand them?"

The citizens of the neighboring cities became very afraid of the sons of Yaakov. They said, "Now they will do to us as they did to these cities."

PEACE AT LAST

All the kings of Canaan wished to make a peace treaty with the Hebrews. On the seventh day after the outbreak of hostilities, Yafia, king of Chevron, sent messengers to the kings of Ai, Giveon, Shalem and Adullam as well as to the kings of Lakish and Chazor — all the kings of the land. "Come to me. We must make a peace pact with the sons of Yaakov. If we do not do this, our entire land will be destroyed. Do not come to me in great numbers. Each one of you should send three of your most important princes and each prince should be accompanied by three servants. Come to Chevron. There we shall meet the sons of Yaakov and discuss terms of peace." They all came as Yafia had requested.

The sons of Yaakov who had heard about this assembly had no faith in their intentions so they remained in Shechem. Meanwhile, twenty-one kings with sixty-three princes and one hundred and eighty-nine servants had assembled at Chevron. The king of Chevron said to them, "Go before us with your men and speak on our behalf. We shall join you and we shall accept whatever terms you make."

The sons of Yaakov sent spies to learn the intention of the kings and to see how many men they were leading. The spies returned with the report that there were only two hundred and eighty-eight men. In the morning, Yaakov and ten of his sons (Yoseif and Binyamin were too young) took sixty-two heavily armed men and set out for Chevron.

Just as they began their journey at the gates of Shechem, Yaakov and his company saw Yafia, king of Chevron, together with their princes and nine men approaching. Yafia approached and bowed to them. Then the sons said, "Why, king of Chevron, have you come to us?" The king answered, "My masters, the kings of Canaan, wish to make peace with you." The brothers still suspected him of deceit. The king, feeling that he was not believed said, "Do you not see that we come in peace; there is no army with us?" Yaakov's men replied, "Send and ask the other kings to come here without any weapons. Then we shall know that they are sincere."

Yafia sent for the other kings who came and bowed and said, "We have heard all that you have done to the Amorites. No person can stand before you. We wish to protect ourselves for the future by making peace with you. Make a covenant with us in peace and in truth. All fighting will then cease."

Then the sons knew that they had come in peace and they heeded their words and made a covenant with them. The princes came with lavish gifts for the sons of Yaakov. Then the kings persuaded the sons of Yaakov to restore the spoil of the seven cities and they did so. They also returned the women and children and the cattle and these were taken back to their native cities.

Then the kings and princes bowed again to the sons of Yaakov. The sons sent them away and they left on peaceful terms. The sons of Yaakov returned to Shechem. From that day on there was peace between the sons of Yaakov and the kings of Canaan. This peace lasted until the Children of Israel returned from Egypt and came to inherit the land of Canaan.

Vayeishev

Yoseif Dreams

At the end of that year, the children of Yaakov made a journey from Shechem to Chevron were Yitzchak was still living. They left their sheep at Shechem because the pastureland there was very good. But now Yaakov and his sons set up their homes in Chevron.

It now happened that in the one hundred and sixth year of the life of Yaakov, that is, ten years after he had returned from Padan Aram, his wife, Leah, died. She was fifty-one years old when she died in Chevron. She was buried in the cave of Machpelah, which had been bought by Avraham from the Chittites.

The sons of Yaakov lived with their father. They had gained fame for their valor. Yoseif and his brother, Binyamin, the two sons of Rachel, were still very young at that time. They had not joined in the battles of their brothers against the Amorites. Yoseif was aware of his brothers' deeds and praised them highly, but he boasted and exalted himself above them. Yaakov loved him dearly, as he was the son of his old age. As a token of his love, he made him a coat of many colors. This coat made him conscious of the fact that he was his father's favorite son, and he brought evil reports of his brothers' actions to his father. The brothers disliked him for these actions and for the love which his father showed him so openly. They were never able to talk with him peacefully. He was seventeen years old but he acted towards his brother in a superior and condescending manner.

He had a dream which he told to his brothers. "I dreamed," he said, "that we were all binding sheaves of corn in the field and my sheaf arose and stood upright and your bundles bowed down to it." The brethren said, "What does this mean? Do you want to be our king? Do you plan to rule over us?" He came to Yaakov and told him his dream and his father kissed him.

Then he dreamed again and told them, "The sun and the moon and eleven stars bowed to me." When Yaakov heard this, he realized the hate-filled atmosphere which these words created in the family. He rebuked Yoseif by saying, "Do you believe that I, your mother and your eleven brothers will come to bow to you?" The brothers were envious and Yaakov took note of these dreams.

One day, the sons of Yaakov were away feeding the sheep near Shechem and delayed returning home. Yaakov was worried, since, with good reason, he suspected that the men of Shechem had planned to renew their war with them. He called Yoseif and said to him, "Are not your brothers with the sheep in Shechem? They have yet to come home. Go and see what has happened to them. See whether they are safe, and let me know."

Yoseif reached Shechem but did not find his brothers there. As he walked about in the fields he saw a stranger who was really an angel sent by God. Yoseif asked the angel, "Have you seen my brothers? Do you know where they are tending sheep?" He told Yoseif, "I overheard them saying that they were going to Dosan." Yoseif then went to Dosan and saw his brothers and walked towards them.

The brothers saw Yoseif coming from a distance and they discussed a plan to kill him. Shimon said, "Look. The dreamer is here. Let us kill him and cast him into a well in the wilderness and tell our father that a wild beast has killed him." Reuven heard this and said, "We must not do this. How will we be able to face our father. Rather, cast him into the pit and let us not be the actual cause of his death." Reuven said this with the intention of saving Yoseif in order to bring him back to his father.

Yoseif came near his brothers and as he sat with them, they rose, threw him down to the ground, stripped him of his coat and cast him into a nearby pit. The pit was empty of water but there were all kinds of horrible snakes and scorpions in it. Yoseif cried, "What are you doing? Why do you not fear God?" God concealed the serpents in the wall of the pit and they did Yoseif no harm.

He called to his brothers, "Yehudah, Reuven, Shimon, and Levi listen to me. What have I done to you? Am I not your own flesh and blood? Why are you doing this to me? How will you ever face our father, Yaakov? You are the descendants of Avraham, Yitzchak and Yaakov, who are famous for their piety and who, with their descendants, would feed strangers and clothe the naked. How much more should you show compassion to your own brother!"

YOSEIF IS SOLD

The brothers moved away from the pit so that they would not have to listen to Yoseif's cries. They sat down to eat a meal and to discuss what to do with him. Then, from afar, they saw a caravan of Yishmaelites traveling in the direction of Egypt. Yehudah said to his brothers, "What will we gain if we kill our own brother. Let us rather sell him to these merchants and, at least, he will end up in some place alive." The brothers agreed but just as they were talking, seven Midianites passed them. They were traders, and they saw the well where Yoseif was. The well was covered by birds who were hovering above it and since the men were very thirsty, they approached the well. They heard Yoseif's cries and when they looked down they saw a handsome young man. They asked him, "Who are you and who placed you in this pit?" They drew him up and took him with them.

Then the brothers saw him with these men. The brothers asked the traders, "What are you doing with our slave? We put him in this pit because of his rebellious nature." The merchants said, "It seems that, on the contrary, you are the servants, since his appearance is so noble. We found him and we shall take him." Then the brothers threatened, "Give us back our slave or we will kill you all." The Midianites drew their swords. Then Shimon leaped towards them bellowing his unearthly yell and they became afraid. He told them, "Not even if you brought all your people with you would you be able to defeat us. We are Yaakov's sons. Now give us back this boy or else your bodies will be eaten by the jackals." Then the strangers consented to buy him and the sons of Yaakov sold Yoseif to them for twenty pieces of silver. Reuven was not with them at that moment.

The Midianites took Yoseif as far as Gilead but they had now regrets about the whole matter. They said, "What have we done. One day we shall be asked about this purchase. Perhaps he was stolen from his father's house and if we are found holding him, we will lose our lives for it." While they were talking, the same company of Yishmaelites which had passed that way before, now passed again and the Midianites tried to rid themselves of the liability and thought of a plan to sell him to this company. They sold Yoseif to the Yishmaelites for 20 pieces of silver and Yoseif was now on the his way to Egypt.

Yoseif cried bitterly when he realized that he was now so far from his home. The company of men were cruel to him. They made him walk long hours on the hot desert sand. When he continued to cry they struck him. But God saw his agony and brought a darkness upon them causing much confusion. The hand of any man who beat Yoseif withered. They proceeded and passed Ephras where Yoseif's mother was buried. Yoseif ran towards the grave and fell on it. He cried, "Mother, wake up from your sleep. See your son who was sold as a slave. Weep with me and fight against these men. Plead my cause before God."

Then as he was on the ground as silent as a stone, he heard a voice speaking to him, "My son, Yoseif, I, Rachel, your mother, hear your cries. I share your sorrow, but have faith in God. He will save you. Go to Egypt and God will be with you there, and will deliver you from all evil."

The men drove him from the grave and he pleaded with them, "Please take me back to my father's house. He will give you a handsome reward." But they argued, "If you really had a father, he would never have sold you at such a low price. No, you are indeed a slave."

The Yishmaelites continued to beat him severely. God sent a strong wind with thunder and lightning and the men did not know where to go. The animals stood motionless. The men knew that they were being punished because of Yoseif. "Pray to God on our behalf," they asked, "and if he forgives us, we will know that all this is happening because of you." He prayed and the frightening noises were no longer heard.

They did not know what to do about Yoseif. One said, "Let us take him back to his father. He will return the money we paid for him." But the distance was now too great to return. They were tempted to go on to Egypt. They said, "There we will get a high price for him. Let us rid ourselves of the trouble this boy is bringing on us." They, therefore, decided to take him to Egypt and dispose of him there.

Regrets

After the brothers had sold Yoseif they suffered much remorse. They wanted to find him and bring him back, but they could not since he had been forced to travel a great distance. Meanwhile, Reuven returned to the pit and descended into it. He cried, "Yoseif, Yoseif" — he heard no reply. He thought, "Surely a snake must have killed him." He rent his garments and said, "The boy is gone — and I, where can I go. How can I bring my father these bad tidings." He told his brothers, "Since I am the oldest son, my father will hold me responsible." They now said that the only thing to do was to find some plausible explanation to give their father. They all took an oath not to disclose the true facts to their father. They swore, "If anyone of us will disclose the true facts, he will be killed by the others."

Then Yisachar advised them to act in the following manner: "Tear the coat which you have taken from Yoseif and then kill a goat. Dip this coat into the blood of the goat. Then our father will understand that Yoseif had been killed by a beast." They did so and gave the coat to Naphtali with a message. "We were gathering our sheep and when we came near Shechem we found this coat." When Yaakov saw the coat, he fell to the ground in a deadly silence. Then he arose and cried, "this is Yoseif's coat!"

As the brothers returned to their homes, they saw their father with torn garments and dust on his head. Yaakov asked them how they had come across the coat. They told him that they had found it near Shechem. Yaakov said, "This is the coat of my son. A wild beast has torn him to pieces." He told the brothers, "I sent him to search for you." They replied, "We did not see him." Yaakov cried, "O Yoseif, I sent you to greet your brothers, and you have been taken from me. How sweet it was when you were with me and how bitter it is with me now. Would that I had died instead of you."

The sons saw their father's distress and they joined him in the mourning. All the sons and their wives and all the servants tried to console Yaakov — without success. The news was told to their grandfather, Yitzchak, who wept with them. He left his home in Chevron and joined his son in order to comfort him. No one could console Yaakov.

Then Yaakov ordered his sons: "Take your weapons and go to the field to retrieve Yoseif's body for burial and search for the first beast you come across." They caught a wolf which they brought to Yaakov saying, "We have not found the body of Yoseif." Yaakov said, "Wolf, why did you kill my son? Why did you not care about my distress?" God opened the mouth of the beast and the wolf said, "What has occurred to you has also occurred to me. My young son has been killed and I have been searching for him for twelve days and cannot find his body, but I swear that I did not kill your son. These man trapped me and in so doing, they added to my grief. Do what you will, but I swear that I have never eaten human flesh." Yaakov sent the beast away and continued to mourn his lost son.

The Yishmaelites who had bought Yoseif from the Midianites came to Egypt. As they approached the border, they met four men of the tribe of Medan, Avraham's son by Keturah. The Yishmaelites offered to sell Yoseif to them and they agreed. They paid nine shekels for him, saying, "We have heard that Potiphar, the captain of Pharaoh's guard, wishes to purchase a good slave."

The Medanites now came to Potiphar's house and said to him, "We have heard that you seek a good slave to serve you. We have one here which we think will be to you liking. If you pay us the price we are asking, he is yours." "Bring him before me," Potiphar said, "that I may see if he pleases me. Then I will pay you what you ask."

Yoseif was brought before Potiphar who was very pleased. He said to them, "Name your price." They told him the sum of twenty silver talents. Potiphar said, "I will pay your price on one condition. Bring before me those who sold him to you. I suspect that he has been kidnapped. This lad is no slave, nor the son of a slave. It is evident by looking at him that he is of a fine and pure lineage.

The Medanites found the group of Yishmaelites who sold Yoseif to them. They swore before Potiphar that Yoseif was indeed a slave. Potiphar accepted their statement and paid the Medanites their price.

Yoseif in Potiphar's House

Potiphar took Yoseif and made him a servant. He was very pleased with him and he became a successful man. God blessed the house of Potiphar on Yoseif's account. Potiphar left all things under Yoseif's supervision and he now became the overseer of all his master's affairs. He was only eighteen years old at that time and there was no person in the whole land as handsome as Yoseif.

Zulikah, Potiphar's wife, saw Yoseif and desired him in her heart. She enticed him daily to be with her but he would not associate with her. She praised his beauty, "You are the most handsome of all men." He would reply, "God has created me like this. This is not due to my own merits. The day will come that I must die like all mortals and this beauty will also die with me." She liked the sound of his voice and asked him, "Come and sing and play the harp for me." Yoseif replied, "I will only sing in praise of God." She offered him a golden comb for his hair. He answered, "Banish these things from your mind." She said, "I could have you bound in irons," but he replied, "God will free me, for He is the One Who unties the bound."

One day, all the women friends of Zulikah came to visit her and they noticed that she was pale and sick. They asked her, "Please tell us what ails you. Why has this pallor come over you?" Instead of answering them, she told her servants, "Prepare a meal for all of the women and place citron fruits and a knife before each guest." Then she had Yoseif clothed in his finest garments and asked that he be brought in while they were eating. As he entered the room, all the women looked up and accidentally cut their hands with the knives without even realizing what they had done.

Then Zulikah laughed, "I give you citron fruit and you cut your hands." They were shocked when they saw blood all over their clothes. They immediately understood why she was so pale and sick. They, in turn, remarked that it was hardly possible to look at such beauty and restrain oneself. They advised her, "Let him know what your innermost feelings are." She told them, "I have already done this, but it is of no avail and I am becoming more and more disconcerted." All they could say was, "You must devise a plan to entice him once and for all."

One day he came to work in the house as usual, when she fell on him, and he was compelled to put her on the ground. She told him, "No one will ever know. You have nothing to fear from your master." He said, "My master left everything to me. I will not allow myself to do such a thing against your husband and thereby sin against God." Yet, Zulikah was not discouraged.

Not long after that, the Nile River overflowed its banks. This was a cause for merry-making and the people went to watch the scene and dance to the music. The whole household of Potiphar joined in the festivities. Only Zulikah did not go out. She feigned sickness so that she could now be alone with Yoseif. She decked herself in her finest clothes and jewels. She perfumed herself with rare fragrance and perfumed the whole house, and sat herself near the door. When Yoseif came into the house to perform his daily duties he saw her at the entrance and tried to avoid her. She seized him by his garments saying, "I swear by the king's life that on this day you will do as I ask or you will die." As she said this, she drew a dagger which she had hidden beneath her garments and put this weapon on his neck. After releasing himself from her grasp he rushed away from her, and in so doing, she tore his garment. Yoseif abandoned his garment with Zulikah and ran from the house.

Zulikah was now afraid that people would discover what had occurred so she removed her fineries and dressed in everyday clothes. She held on to Yoseif's upper garment which she had torn from him. She then asked a servant to summon the members of the household. When they arrived she cried out, "See what your master has done to me. He brought a Hebrew slave to make sport with me. When he saw that I was alone in the house he came towards me with evil intentions. I cried for help and he escaped in fear. This is his cloak which he left behind on fleeing."

The servant reported at once to Potiphar who came quickly. Zulikah told him too, "What do you mean by bringing the Hebrew slave to defile me?" Yoseif was then brought before Potiphar and beaten. "Oh God," Yoseif prayed,"You know that I am innocent of this charge. Why should I die at the hands of these heathens?"

There was a child in the house of Potiphar who was only eleven months old. God suddenly gave it the power of speech and the child cried, "This is all false. Why do you punish him. Zulikah speaks lies against Yoseif." The child described everything which he had witnessed. Upon hearing this, Potiphar felt ashamed. The beating of Yoseif ceased but Potiphar still brought the innocent

Yoseif before the priest-judge. Yoseif pleaded innocent to the charges. The decision of the judges was that the garment be brought for investigation. They ruled: "If the cloak is torn in the front part, it will prove that Zulikah had seized Yoseif and had acted with cunning." The coat was brought and so it was found. The tear was in the front. Yoseif was acquitted of the charge, but in order to protect Zulikah's reputation, he was put in prison all the same.

Yoseif was assigned to the same prison in which the king's prisoners were kept. He was to be there for twelve months. Even here, Zulikah continued to pursue him. She came there daily and offered to free him if he would only submit to her. "It is far better to be here," Yoseif said, "than to be enticed to sin by you!" She threatened to have him put in irons but even this did not move him. She finally ceased talking to him.

All this time Yoseif's father, Yaakov, and his brothers in Canaan were mourning for him.

GENERATIONS

In the same year that Yoseif was brought to Egypt, Reuven went to a place called Timna and took a wife, Alyuram, daughter of Chavi the Canaanite. She gave birth to four sons: Chanoch, Pallu, Chezron and Karmi. Shimon had five sons: Nemuel, Yamin, Ohad, Yachin and Tzochar. Then with Bunah, whom he had taken from Shechem, he had a son, Shaul. Yehudah went to Adullam and lived near an Adullamite named Chiram. There he saw Alis the daughter of a Canaanite man named Shua. She bore him sons: Eir, Onan and Sheilah.

Yisachar and Levi went to the east country and married the daughters of Yovav, son of Yoktan, son of Ever. Yovav had two daughters. The older one was Adinah and the younger, Aridah. Levi married Adinah and Yisachar married Aridah. These wives were brought back to Canaan. Levi's wife bore Gershon, Kehas and Merori. Aridah, wife of Yisachar bore Tola, Puvah, Yov and Shimron.

Dan went to Moav and married Aflalet, daughter of Chamidan. For some time, she bore no children until finally a son was born called Chushim. Gad and Naftali went to Charan and married the daughters of Amuran, son of Utz, son of Nachor. The older daughter was Merimas and the younger, Utzis. Naphtali took Merimas and Gad took Utzis. Naphtali's sons were Yachtze'el, Guni, Yietzer and Shillem. Gad's sons were Tzifyoni, Chaggi, Shuni, Etzbon, Eiri, Arodi and Areili.

Asher married Adon, daughter of Ephlal, son of Hadad, son of Ishmael, but she died at that time without children. Asher then went and married a woman from across the river, Hadorah, daughter of Avimael, son of Ever, son of Shem. Hadorah was very comely and intelligent and had been married to Malkiel, son of Eilam, son of Shem and had borne the latter a daughter named Serach. When her husband, Malkiel, died, Hadorah returned to her father and then Asher, whose wife had died, now married her. She brought her daughter, Serach, with her to Canaan when the child was three and Asher raised her in Yaakov's house. She was like a daughter to Asher, and God gave her great wisdom. Then Hadorah bore sons to Asher: Yimnah, Yishvah, Yishvi and Beriah.

Zevulun went to Medan to marry Marosha, daughter of Molad, son of Avida, son of Midian. She bore him Sered, Eilah and Yachle'el.

Yaakov sent to Aram, son of Tzova, son of Terach and obtained a wife for Binyamin, his son. He was only ten years old at the time and he married Machalya, daughter of Charam. She bore him Bela, Becher, Ashbel, Gera and Na'aman. Then Binyamin took Arvas, daughter of Zimran, son of Avraham (by Keturah) when he was eighteen and she bore him Eichi, Rosh, Muppin, Chuppin and Ard.

At that time, Yehudah went to the house of Shem and took Tamar, daughter of Eilam, son of Shem for his oldest son, Eir. But

Eir acted in an unseemly manner and he perished. Yehudah told Onan to marry his brother's wife. He did so, but sinned and died. Yehudah now told his daughter-in-law to wait in widowhood until his third son, Sheilah, would be old enough to marry. Yehudah, however, was afraid that Sheilah, too, might perish. Tamar then waited in her father's house for some time.

Now Yehudah's wife, Alis, died and he went together with his friend, Chirah, to shear the sheep at Timna. Tamar knew about this and she removed her widow's garments and put a veil over her face. She sat at Pesach Einayim on the road to Timna. Yehudah, not knowing who she was, took her. She bore twins from him — their names were Peretz and Zerach.

THE PRISONERS' DREAM

Yoseif was still in prison in Egypt. At that time, two of Pharaoh's officers, the "supervisor of the wine-cellar" and the "supervisor of the bakery" were in the prison. It was Yoseif's duty to attend to their needs. The wine butler's job was to take a cup of wine and place it before Pharaoh while the head baker placed the bread and pastry before him. The princes and officers who ate at the king's table once noticed a fly in Pharaoh's cup of wine and a pebble in his bread. The two officers were immediately condemned to prison and awaited judgment. Yoseif attended these officers for a whole year. At the end of the year it happened that both the butler and chief baker had a dream during the same night and the dreams troubled them so that they were manifestly worried in the morning. Yoseif asked them why they were so troubled and they both told him that they each had a disturbing dream. They could find no one who could interpret these dreams. Yoseif offered his services as interpreter of the dreams.

The butler related his dream which was as follows: "There was a tall vine-tree from which shot out three branches. These produced beautiful blossoms. Then clusters were seen which ripened and became grapes. I took the grapes and pressed them into

Pharaoh's cup and the king drank of it." "The dream is a good omen," Yoseif explained. "The three branches signify three days. In three days' time, you will be freed and restored to your former office." Yoseif did, however, ask the butler, "Remember me in the good days when you will have been restored to your office because I am an innocent man. I have been taken from the land of the Hebrews and committed to prison for no reason."

Now that the butler had his dream explained in such a happy manner, the baker, too, asked Yoseif to explain his dream. In his dream he had been carrying three wicker baskets on his head with all manner of pastry in the top basket which was being pecked at by the birds as he was carrying it on his head. "The three baskets," Yoseif said, "signify three days. In three days from now you will be hanged and that fowl will eat your flesh."

Three days later a son was born to Pharaoh — his first-born. The king made a great banquet for all his servants which lasted a week. The butler was restored to his former dignity and the baker was put to death. The butler, however, forgot about Yoseif and the latter remained in prison for two more years. This punishment was from God. Yoseif should have trusted God and not relied on the butler.

Yitzchak, son of Avraham, was still alive at this time and he lived to the age of one hundred and eighty. His son, Eisav, was in Edom where he took possession of the land, together with the sons of Seir. Eisav learned that his father was nearing his end and he came to Canaan. Yaakov and his sons left their dwellings to come to Yitzchak, while Yaakov continued mourning for his son, Yoseif. Yitzchak asked that the eleven sons of Yaakov come near to him so that he could bless them. He embraced each of them and said, "May the God of your fathers bless you and increase your offspring as the stars of the heaven." He also blessed the sons of Eisav by saying, "May God put the fear of you in the hearts of your enemies." He then called Yaakov and Eisav and said, "The God of the whole earth spoke to me and told me that this land would be given to my children only if they observe His laws, and then He, too, would keep the covenant which He had made with Avraham. Teach your sons and their children to fear God and to walk in the good ways." Having ended this blessing, Yitzchak died. Yaakov and Eisav fell on their father and they wept. They took him and buried him in the cave of Machpelah. All the kings of Canaan went with Yaakov and Eisav, and the sons of Yaakov walked barefooted until they reached Kiryas Arba. Yitzchak was buried with great honors, as a king would have been buried.

When Yitzchak died, he left all his possessions to his sons. Eisav said to Yaakov, "Give me my share of what our father left us! We shall divide it between us." Yaakov agreed to this and brought everything and placed it all in front of his brother. He then addressed Eisav as follows. "The God of heaven and earth told our fathers, Avraham and Yitzchak, that He would give this land to their children as an inheritance. Which will you now take? If you choose the land, I shall take the possessions and if you take the material wealth, I shall take the land for me and my children after me for all time." Nevayos, the son of Yishmael, was present at this meeting. Eisav now asked Nevayos for his advice. Nevayos said, "What question do you ask? Do you not see for yourself that all the sons of Canaan dwell on this land very securely? How can you talk of inheriting it? Take the wealth which is before you and leave the land to your brother, Yaakov." Eisav took the advice of Nevayos and he received the wealth which consisted of servants, cattle, and all other material goods. But Yaakov took the land from the river of Egypt to the Euphrates for his children for all time. Also the Cave of Machpelah was written over to Yaakov. All this was written in a deed with witnesses.

This is the text of the document:

> The Land of Canaan and all the cities of the Chittites, Yevusites, Amorites and Perizzites — all the seven nations from the River of Egypt to the Euphrates — the whole city of

> Chevron-Kiryas Arba and the cave in that territory has been acquired by Yaakov from Eisav, his brother, as a possession.

Yaakov took this deed and placed the document in an earthen vessel. He gave it to his sons. Eisav took all the wealth that his father had left him and returned to Seir. He took his place among the inhabitants of that land and remained there from that day onward. So the whole of the Land of Canaan became the inheritance of the Children of Israel, while Eisav and his sons inherited Mount Seir.